Scribbles
on the
Restroom Wall

Scott Shaw

BUDDHA ROSE PUBLICATIONS

Scribbles on the Restroom Wall
Copyright © 2011 by Scott Shaw
All Rights Reserved.
www.scottshaw.com

Rear cover photograph of Scott Shaw
by Hae Won Shin
Copyright © 2011 All Rights Reserved.

This book contains material protected under International and Federal Copyright Laws and Treaties. Any unauthorized reprint or use of this material is prohibited. No part of this book may be reproduced or transmitted in any form or by any means, electronic or mechanical, including photocopying, recording, or by any information storage and retrieval system without express written permission from the author or publisher.

First Edition

ISBN: 1-877792-53-5
ISBN 13: 9781877792533

Library of Congress Control Number:
2011933494

Printed in the United States of America

10 9 8 7 6 5 4 3 2 1

Scribbles
on the Restroom Wall

Contents

Introduction	**9**
Only If I Had To…	**17**
And Now What?	**19**
Shiva Verses Saraswati	**20**
Diplomatic Immunity	**22**
Identity	**24**
Enlightenment or Insanity?	**27**
Catching the Ego	**29**
STOP POLLUTING FOR NO REASON!!!	**31**
Get a Life!	**33**
What Are You Thinking?	**39**
Consciously Doing or Doing Consciously	**41**
Zen and the Void	**43**
The World Didn't End! Again…	**45**
The Dojang Experience	**47**
The Spirituality of Doing	**50**
Justice	**52**
Do Your Business	**55**
You Ruined My Life!	**57**
In the Waning Days of Vinyl	**60**
Gentlemen Remove Their Hats	**62**
Migraine	**64**
Got Any Change?	**68**
Lemon Ice Cubes	**69**
Fantasy	**74**
Stop Blaming Others for the Mistakes You Make!	**72**

Howl	**75**
How Long Do Pillowcases Last?	**77**
Artistic Inclination	**78**
"I Coulda' Been a Contender."	**81**
Look Before You Leap...	**83**
Zen and Me	**86**
Process Verses Insanity	**88**
Only Human	**90**
The Process	**92**
Keep Your Feet Off of the Table!	**94**
Nature	**96**
How We See Ourselves	**98**
Loudmouth Loser	**100**
Part of the Process	**102**
This is Reality	**104**
Right Turn Only	**105**
No Outcome	**106**
Seeking	**108**
You Will Forget This Moment	**111**
Out of the Body into the What?	**113**
What's In It for Me?	**116**
The Stories You Will Never Know	**119**
Make Things Better!	**121**
The Art Has Been Done	**122**
Remembering When	**123**
Everybody's Got the Same Hustle	**124**
Arrogance	**127**
Human Beings are very self-centered creatures	**130**

Be Willing to Change Your Ideologies	**133**
You Only Get One Shot	**135**
Step Up to the Plate	**137**
Liar	**141**
Don't Psychoanalyze Me!	**144**
Ark Yuey Wong: To Fight or Not to Fight?	**147**
We All Make a Deal with the Devil	**150**
Don't Keep Your Horses in Cages!	**152**
The Only Bad Movies I'm In Are My Own	**154**
The Scott Shaw Guide to International Travel	**156**
Buddha on the Net	**163**
Comfort Women	**165**
Rules of the Road	**168**
I'm a Nuclear Boy in the Nuclear World	**170**
Change is Not Always for the Better	**172**
Filmmaking: Keeping the Artist from Creating Art	**174**
They Can Say Anything...	**177**
Don't Talk to the Help	**181**
Do Something	**186**
Influences	**188**
Hoarding	**191**
Oblivious	**196**
Selling Your Religion	**199**
It's All About the Benjamins, Baby!	**201**
Trapped By Circumstance	**203**
You Never Know Who You Never Knew That You Knew	**207**
The Learning Annex	**210**

No Rehearsals	**215**
You Can Only Play In Your Own Playground	**217**
GET OUT OF THE FAST LANE!	**222**
Locked Into Your Own Mind	**224**
Stealing and Selling Other People's Work	**227**
I'll Have a Scott Shaw	**230**
Don't be a Wait-er	**232**
What's Wrong with Humanity?	**234**
Who's Right?	**238**
Anybody Can Do That!	**241**
Trying	**242**
The Martial Arts	**245**
Born in the U.S.A.	**248**
Don't Cry Over Spilled...	**250**
How Quickly We Forget	**251**
Racial Slurs	**253**
Fractured	**256**
The Party	**258**
Keith and Kenny	**261**
Drama Queen	**263**
The Commune	**266**
Monkey Wrench in the Gears	**269**

Introduction

I began writing a blog and posting it to my website in early 2011. I truly enjoyed the process. It was a great way to present my thoughts, ideals, feelings, and experiences in a concise manner. Soon after I began blogging the problems began. But, I will get to those in a moment...

Ever since I was a young boy, I enjoyed reading biographies and autobiographies. Certainly, books like, *Autobiography of a Yogi*, were a great influence on my spiritual development. I also enjoyed reading about people's lives in magazines. As I got older, I was drawn to the literary writings of authors who embraced the first-person in the telling of their tales. I felt this style of storytelling truly brought the reader into the mind of the central character. The interest in the actual workings of humanity also made me a fan of Reality T.V.—long before it was ever called Reality. T.V.

For those of you who are old enough, or for those of you who wish to look back into the archives of television history, there was a television show called, *Dragnet*. This series was based on true criminal events that were acted out on the screen. As a child, I enjoyed the show.

A funny story... Each episode of *Dragnet* began with the lead character, Joe Friday, stating, "This is the city, Los Angeles, California..." As a young boy, being from Los Angeles, I assumed that they made the show for every city; at least every major city. When I went to visit my mother's hometown in the Midwest one summer, when I was about six, I was watching T.V. one evening and was quite surprised to find out that it was the same show, *"This is the city, Los Angeles, California. The stories you will see are true. The names have been changed to protect the innocent"* They didn't make episodes for every city! Awh, the mind of a child... ☺

Later came the birth of true Reality T.V. The ongoing documentary series, COPS has remained one of my favorite television shows. It also became one of my primary influences as a filmmaker. Then, shows like, The Real World on MTV and various, *"Reality T.V."* offshoots became the norm in the late twentieth century. This trend has amplified into the twenty-first century.

Perhaps Reality T.V. has fueled it, but whatever the cause, society has become very hungry for fame. Everybody wants to be famous for doing or achieving absolutely nothing. In fact, I have known several people who have attempted to launch their own reality series and place their shows on sites like YouTube. In this same era, vlogging has become quite commonplace.

I quickly saw the problems with this trend. Those who were doing their own reality shows and vlogs were allowing people, that they did not know, into the inner workings of their lives. As such, it has become quite common, especially for women who have pursued this path, to develop stalkers and to have other strange deviant types of crazed people, who inhabit this modern world, driven by the Internet, to follow their every move and read completely deluded self-driven falsehoods into their every word. As such, I always warned people I knew who were following this road to be very-very-very careful. I guess I should have listened to my own advice...

Which brings me back to the main point of this discourse; namely, my blog.

Though the primary purpose of my blog was to investigate human consciousness. Very soon after the inception of the blog situations began to occur to me.

As it was my blog, I would intermingle discussions on consciousness with my own human experiences and interactions. What occurred from this process became quite, (for lack of a better term), curious... For example, I would mention a place where I liked to eat or have coffee. The next time I would arrive at this location there would be some wide-eyed person sitting across the courtyard staring at me. In some cases, people would come up to me and ask to take a photograph with me or get my autograph. The photographs were fine but as I do not do the autograph thing, some people became upset.

Amusingly, in one blog I mentioned this restaurant that I frequent. As I was walking in the door of the restaurant the next day, this girl comes running up. She obviously wanted to enter the doorway before me. I happily held the door open for her. She then turned to me and said, *"Wow, aren't you Scott Shaw? You eat here?"*

Surprise-Surprise. Fancy meeting you here... ☺

She continued, *"Here's my headshot. Maybe you can use me in your next film..."*

This was all very flattering, but it also made me become a bit worried about what other types of unseen stalking was taking place in my life due to the blog. Stalking, that I did not notice or was not alerted to.

This stalking trend continued onto the Internet. People were reading my blog and realizing that I would discuss and reflect upon situations that happened to me. From this, there was a small group of people, (with no life and nothing better to do, I guess), who would do things like e-mail me and say something really stupid or lie about me on some website, just to see if they could get a rise out of me, so that I would mention them in my blog. As I do not patrol the Internet, and hardly have the time or the inclination to do so, some person, who probably thought they were doing me a favor, would inevitably e-mail me about these statements, *"Did you see what this person wrote about you on that site?"*

Inevitably, as I detail in one of the blogs in this book, this was just somebody's method to get their fifteen minutes of fame and gain it via me. Again, they were attempting to gain notoriety while doing nothing to create it for themselves. Nothing, but insulting me... How ridiculous is that?

Personally, I found this all supremely amusing. I mean, how can you insult or criticize a person who doesn't care about what you have to say? But, I did feel for these people. I mean what a supreme waste of life. And, life is so-so short.

Initially, I continued blogging but cut out the references to people who were directly interactive with my present. It didn't really work, however. People kept trying to find new ways to come at me.

As a human being, I have always been very open and up-front. I speak the truth, as I know it. I say what I feel. If someone asks me a question, I answer it in the most direct and honest manner possible. This is how I operated my blog. What occurred from this, however, was that it allowed all those adolescents and adolescent minded people the ability to attempt to push my buttons.

If they actually knew me, they would know that my buttons don't easy get pushed. None-the-less, I found all of these attempts geared towards me to be quite childish and foolish. Like I detail in the aforementioned blog presented in this book, where I addressed these situations, *"Get a life!"* But, as everyone continues to seek fame, by any means necessary, people didn't take the hint.

As you can image, I am a very busy person. As such, I just do not have the time to deal with that style of nonsense in my life. Nor do I need to be thinking about what may come next. So, in early June 2011, I ended the blog. At the point I ended the blog, I received numerous questions, *"Why?"* I also received numerous requests to recommence. These questions and requests obviously came from the nice and the friendly people—the ones who were actually reading the blog and were interested in what I had to say. These comments were not, however, from those who were haunting the blogosphere and hunting me down.

So, simply as a means of self-preservation, I stopped writing the blog—at least until I can afford to have a whole security team around me and a team to patrol the Internet. I'm joking, of course, as that is not the kind of person that I am.

Finally, you may wonder about the title of this book, *"Scribbles on the Restroom Wall."*

Do you ever notice how gang members write their name and list their gang affiliations on the walls of dirty public restrooms? I have even seen their names scratched into toilet seats. If you ask me, that never seemed like a very appealing place for people to find your name referenced.

In times gone past, before the world became so *gangsta*, people would draw pictures and sometimes write a foolish joke, a poem, or a bit of abstract musings on the restroom walls. Again, not a great place for art, but somehow it does seem like an ironically appropriate place for misguided philosophy.

    I was in a public restroom a couple of weeks ago and the inspiration for the title came to me. Initially, I was simply going to use it as subject matter for a blog. But, as I pretty much put all my thoughts on the subject into the last few sentences, I guess I don't need to make it an entire blog entry. But, it does still make for a catchy title for this book.

    So, there you have it: the foundations for this book and the inspiration for the title. That's the story... For those of you who enjoyed the blog or for those of you who did not yet get the opportunity to read it, here it is in its entirety; just as it was posted on scottshaw.com up until June of 2011. It is presented just as I wrote it. I even left in all of the original typos. I have also added a number of additional blog entries to those that were originally posted. I did this for those of you who were reading the blog to get some new grist for the mill.

    I trust you will find these writings interesting, informative, enjoyable, and in some cases humorous. And please, if you want to communicate with me or meet me, I am the easiest person in the world to contact. You don't have to stalk me, nor do you have to insult me if you want to carry on a conversation.

God Bless...
Scott Shaw
15 June 2011

Scribbles on the Restroom Wall

_____Only If I Had To...

I was speaking with the lady last night. She was a very pretty, upscale woman. She got talking about when she was younger, she made her living as a stripper. This guy asked her, *"Would you ever do that again?"* She immediately and emphatically said, *"No."* Then, you could tell that she became very reflective for a moment and said, *"Only if I had too..."*

This is the thing with life, *"Only if I had to..."* We all do things that the wish we hadn't done or we wish we did not have to do. This is the curse of life, if you will.

There are all these years of our life and there are a million things coming at us at all times. And, to survive; we must do things that we really don't want to do—simply to survive.

On the other side of the issue there is all of the things that are presented to us that we should/that we must own. It was in the news yesterday that a young boy in the People's Republic of China sold one of his kidneys to buy an Apple iPod2. Are you kidding me! What about when the next Apple iPod comes out? Or the one he bought breaks?

People are sucked into the illusion of need. But, they enter this place of need with no discretion. They do it because they are told that they need. Thus, they believe that they need. But, with no clear perception of life-reality, they are lead down a road that can never be altered.

I frequently meet young people in their twenties. They ask about me and my life, so I ask about theirs. I always expect them to say, *"I'm going to college."* Or, *"I working towards this or that..."* In some cases, this is their story. But, in more cases than not, this is not their story at all. They are simply pursuing nothing—willing to accept the nothing. They are willing to perform the most menial of jobs and have no focus on the future.

Usually, at this stage, I do not ask them any further questions, as I do not want to put them on the spot. But, it always makes me wonder what they expect that they will be doing when they get to their thirties or forties, like the woman I was speaking with last evening.

The main thing about life is that there are no guarantees. No matter what you do, no matter what prerequisites you undertake, they do not guarantee an outcome. But, what foundational building blocks you lay today, for your future tomorrow, whether it is study or a focused pursuit towards your idealized end goal, keeps you from ever contemplating, *"Only if I had too..."*

And Now What?

Life is defined by action. What you do leads to the definition of your life.

Most people do not think about what they do. They just do it. They may be guided by friends, family, cultural trends, desires, or necessity. But, at the end of the day, they have done what they have done, and are thereby defined by the consequences.

The other side of the coin is that some people do, very consciously, think about what they are doing. Even though this is the case, they do what they do defined by the same previous criteria: friends, family, cultural trends, desires, or necessity. The problem arises in the fact that though they thought about it and decided that they wanted to do it, (whatever IT may be), they never thought about the final outcome. From this lack of forethought, they are again defined by the consequences of their action that they, themselves, set in motion.

This is one of the main points of living a conscious life. You must first understand that we all do what we do. That's just life... But, we also must understand is that what we do has consequences. That's karma.

The question is, *"You did what you and now what?"*

Shiva Verses Saraswati

The Hindu god Shiva is known as the destroyer, the lord of destruction. Though it is believed that his powers are ideally geared towards removing ignorance, his essence is that of destruction.

The Hindu goddess Saraswati is the goddess of music and the arts. She is the essence of creativity. She is the muse; the source for all that is good and creative in the world.

Most people do not create. Yet, the try to tear down, criticize, and diminish the creations of those who do. How many times have you heard someone saying, *"That's shit."* Or, *"Anybody can do that."* But, as I often say, these people do not do, they simply criticize. They follow the path of Shiva.

On the other hand, those who do create, see the beauty in all things they view and appreciate all of this world as art; be it music, paintings, sculpture, cinema, photography, all the way to how a person dresses or how they wear their hair. To the creative person, they see all things as art, and, thus, are continually surround by beauty, positivity, and creativity.

No matter where you find yourself in life or what is dominating your emotions and your personality, you can choose to follow the path of Saraswati and shun the path of Shiva. Because here is the simple fact that has been proven over-and-over in this place we call LIFE, if you follow the path of destructive negativity, then negativity will always seek you out and hinder anything that you do. If, on the other hand, you follow the path of positive creativity then positivity will always find you; you will find your muse and be guided whenever you need help—positive spiritual guidance will always be at hand.

Life is very simple, and life is very obvious. It is you who chooses what you do with it.

Diplomatic Immunity

I met and spent some quality time with this very nice girl in Kuala Lumpur, (KL to the locals), back in the late 1980s. I eventually hit on back to L.A. She planned to come and spend some time with me here, but I guess due to the fact that it was difficult to get a visa, she never made it. I also planned to go back, as at that point in my life, virtually every month I was traveling in Asia. We spoke on the phone several times but then my life got involved with the film industry. This became all-consuming, so time passed.

She called me one-day and I heard some very sad news. She had been at this club, (actually the club where we had met), with some friends and a Saudi guy asked her to dance. She turned him down, so he broke his glass on the bar and cut her face. Even sadder, she had this condition where any cut to her body swelled up and scarred very badly. So, she was obviously pretty devastated.

She took the matter to the police, but the guy had diplomatic immunity, so they did nothing. Moreover, she was of Chinese heritage.

For those of you who may not know this, in Malaysia, and other Asian Islamic countries for that matter, the large indigenous Chinese population is really looked down upon; they are really the second-class citizens, as they are not Muslim. So, the police did nothing to the man, he just went on his way, and she was left scarred for life.

In the news media, due to all of the political changes that are rapidly taking place in the Middle East, it is often discussed how the men are the very dominate figures of their society and how they physically and mentally abuse women with no repercussions. In fact, the women are the ones who are blamed if anything negative happens to them. This is true. And, it is a very sad illustration of world society and how, in fact, very little has changed in the overall landscape of human evolutionary consciousness.

    I have often wondered how this girl's life may have evolved differently for her if she could have just made it to L.A.

Identity

We each have our own identity. We see ourselves in a certain way and we wish to present that image to the world. Though this image may change and evolve over the years, it is a unique quality defined solely by ourselves.

When we are young this self-image is more influx. At that stage of our lives, we are more easily influenced by society and, thus, are more willing to shift and to adapt to be accepted by whatever society and group of friends we find ourselves surround by. I have a friend who believes that men set the standard for who they are and how they want to be seen in junior high school and then never really change. Maybe... In the case of women, it is obvious that they are more willing to change as they commonly change their hair and clothing style throughout their life. But, though these external images may change, women also have a view of their inner-self that maintains a constant—an ideology that they wish to project to the world.

It must be understood that the outer-self is a projection of the inner-self. And, this is where problems arise. I remember when I was in 9th grade, there was this guy who had the nicest and longest, long hair, all throughout junior high school. That was a time in history when a man having long hair actually stood for something. In any case, he got a job at a fast-food restaurant during the summer and had to cut his hair. When we would go and visit him, all he could talk about was the fact that he didn't feel like himself any longer.

This is the problem with external image; it becomes convoluted with internal image and ego comes into play. People move from simply illustrating who they are, to constructing something that they want to be viewed by the world. It no longer is an illustration of self-image; instead, it becomes a projection of ego. In other words, it is no longer self, it is an ego driven creation. This is why many spiritual sects have the aspirants shave their heads and wear very plain clothing. But... That too is a projected image that many people aspire to. From that image, they are seen and believed to be holy.

So, what is the answer? All anyone can be is who they are. The fact of the matter is, the majority of the world's population is ego-driven. As such, they present themselves in a manner defined by their personal ego. Don't get me wrong, the fact of the matter is, many who walk the spiritual path fall into this pattern, as well. Perhaps the most confounding problem with this evaluation is the fact that many people do not even know who they truly are. They have been defined by their friends, their family, their society, and so on. They were never allowed to truly explore themselves and become who they truly are. Thus, whatever image is projected, is not a pure and true image.

The answer... Stop behaving in a manner that is not you. Look deep and find out who you truly are. Most of us are very nice, kind people inside. We are not power hungry, negative, or seductive people. If we have behaved like that, though this internal quest, the source of this attitude may be found, and you may discover that person is not who you truly are at all. It may take some doing but instead of living an ego-based existence you can reemerge as a positive force and present a positive image to the world. From this, not only you, but everything becomes better.

_____Enlightenment or Insanity?

There is this guy that I have seen walking around in various cities around where I live for the past ten or fifteen years. He has short grey hair. He is clean-shaven. He always wears white dungarees and a white tee shirt. Both are usually soiled and a little dirty. Sometimes, like when I saw him today, he is carrying a large drink, like a Big Gulp from 711 in his hand. He walks very fast, and inevitably is ranting and raving, howling to the moon if you will, about something. Something, I know not what, as I have never been close enough to him to hear what he is actually saying.

Is he insane? Probably... But, he obviously lives somewhere in the vicinity and he has for many years. So, he is at least somewhat functional.

Here in the States, and in most of the civilized world, for that matter, when we see someone like this, the word, *"Crazy,"* comes to mind. But, this is simply our perception, our perimeters of reality. If this guy were in India, he may very well be thought to be an enlightened saint. As I have long said, *"In India, the crazier you are, the holier you are."*

In India, they have a very different sense of perception and reality than we do in the West. All one needs to do is to look at the life and the behavior of the revered East Indian Sage, Sri Ramakrishna, to confirm this fact. I won't go into it here, as you can find this information in a lot of other places; but, by western standards, he was quite mad. One of his quirks what that he continually called out to his mother. The divine mother, so it was believed. Thus, he was considered a saint. By today's standards, he may have simply been medicated and there would have gone his ethereal communications, and thus his sainthood. But, he was allowed to relish in his own reality. And, instead of being shunned by society, as may have happened if he had lived in the West, he was embraced as a true knower. So much so, that his disciples set the stage for much of the Hindu/yogic philosophy that moved from the East to the West.

It must be understood, it is fine line between insanity and enlightenment. For the most part, it is simply the way a specific individual is perceived by the culture where he (or she) finds themselves. Just because we all accept specific lines of defined reality and sanity, that does not make them true or right, they are simply what we have been taught to believe.

Enlightened or Insane, it is a hard definition to know for certain...

Catching the Ego

People who walk the spiritual path are taught to be very conscious of their ego. This is true of people who are schooled in some of the various new-school psychological refinement methods, as well. This, however, is not the case for most of the rest of this planet's population.

People want to look in the mirror and feel good about themselves. They want to wear clothing in a specific styling. They want their hair styled in a specific and trendy look. They want the girls or the guys to check them out. They want to be found attractive. They want to have money, position, power, rank, and title. When they do accomplish any of these, even in small quantities, they flaunt it all around. For those who don't achieve this, they lie about the fact and pretend to be something more than what they have actually achieved.

Simply by this definition, I think we can each see the flaws in pursuing the world of ego. It is for this reason that those walking the path of consciousness are taught the ego only gets you into trouble. It leads you down a road that you do not want to be dominated by.

Now, this is not to say that you should be messy, dirty, or never pursue your goals. What this is to say is that you should not be dominated by these factors. And, more so, you must not flaunt anything you may own or achieve. The reason for this is because if you do, in time, you will fall. Why? Because this is the rule of life. There is always a faster gunfighter. There will always be someone stronger, prettier, younger, or more intelligent than you. If all you do is relish in your worldly accomplishments, you WILL fall and it WILL hurt.

On the other hand, if you do what you do, and just do it, then the things in life will come and go as they may, but you will not be dominated or injured by their loss. Someone with better clothing comes along, you can admire it. Someone younger and prettier passes you by, you do not become envious. Someone who has accomplished more than you enters your life, you are not jealous. You are simply WHOLE in who you are at any given stage of your life, and you do not need to enter into the foolish competitions of the ego driven, *"I am this and you are not..."*

Catch yourself. Let go of your ego. It will leave you mush more happy and much more free. And probably, with more money in your bank account.

STOP POLLUTING FOR NO REASON!!!

Last Tuesday I was coming out of a shop on Pacific Coast Highway and a guy walking in front of me had just finished the water he was drinking out of a plastic bottle. He looked at it and threw it on the ground. WHAT!!!

I spend the last few days up North. I was sitting in a window seat at the *Starbucks* on Kearney Street, in San Francisco, with a lady friend of mine, drinking a cafe misto. I observed as this young lady took a few long drags off of her cigarette and then threw the butt on the ground. A few minutes later I see a guy pull his bike up to the curb, light up a smoke, take a few drags, throw the butt on the ground, and ride off. Within the next few minutes, I see several other people throw their smoked cigarettes on the ground. All be it that in San Francisco people smoke much more than they do in many other cities... But, ARE YOU KIDDING ME!!!

As I write this, I think back to a couple of years ago when I was following behind a limousine and the driver, apparently done with his Subway style sandwich, opens his window and simply tosses the remains of it, in its plastic bag, out his window. I slammed on my horn and left it on for a very long time.

When I was a kid, I remember the commercials that were on T.V. that said, *"Every litter bit hurts."* Later there was the commercials and billboards, *"Give a hoot, don't pollute."*

I think most people get it. They really try to keep things clean and make this decaying planet at least a little bit better. Then, there are those who are so wrapped up in their own momentary reality that they just don't care. It really surprises me when people behave like this. I mean we can all do small things to make things better. We can also do small things to make things much worse.

Recently, I have noticed a few commercials on T.V. and I have seen a few news specials about how much pollution occurs when people toss their cigarettes onto the ground, as they get swept or washed into the sewer systems and end up in the rivers or oceans where most sewer systems feed. Do smokers think about this? I think most do not. They are the worst polluters. They just want to feed their very bad and disgusting habit and then toss away their discards; never being conscious enough to care about what happens. They're killing themselves for no good reason, why should they care what they do to others or to this planet?

So, what's the answer? YOU must make a difference where you can. This nonchalant, *"Just fuck everything,"* attitude is simply wrong, immature, and stupid. Do the right thing and fix what you, I, and the rest of humanity have broken. STOP POLLUTING FOR NO REASON!!!

Get a Life!

As you can imagine, me being who I am, I have had my share of stalkers. In each case, it is not a very good experience. So, I can really feel for the real celebrities out there, who have to deal with it on a much larger scale.

I always find it sadly amusing when people stalk someone, whether it be physically or on the Internet. I find that almost universally they do this because they are, for lack of a better term, jealous. They do it because they have no life so they attempt to make a name for themselves by doing something to someone else who has achieved some form of notoriety.

And, this is the sad fact of life, the minute you accomplish anything, there are going to be those detractors who will try to diminish your accomplishments. They do this in order to make themselves feel like they are something more. Like I say to everybody who has criticized me, *"If you don't like what I've done, stop wasting your time criticizing me; get out there, and do something better."* I have never seen this happen, however. I have heard a lot of claims that it will happen, but nothing ever does.

There have been more than a few women who have refused to let go and have stalked me. But, I have more sympathy for them. As women commonly believe love is the cure-all for everything, they find it hard to let go. But, believe me, it is not...

In the more purely stalker since, here are a couple of stalking examples that have occurred to me which you might find interesting. It is important to note, however, that these are only a couple of the examples that I have encountered with stalkers. Sadly, there has been several others.

At one point in my life, whenever I would leave my car parked outside, inevitably, something weird would go wrong with it. A wire would be disconnected, my brake-line would be spouting fluid, the lug nuts on a tire would be loosened, or my oil pan bolt would be loose, and I would be dripping oil. This went on for a little while until I realized that it was being done by one of my, *"So-called friends."* This guy always spoke about his jealously for the accomplishments of other people. But, it took me a while to realize that it was him, a guy who I considered a friend, actually messing with me. I mean, this guy came from money, had a great job; he could have done anything with his life. But instead, he chose to waste his life doing nonsense like that. What a waste! Me, I quit parking my car on the street.

Another couple of interesting stalker situation occurred due to my involvement in the martial arts.

There was this guy who, more than once, cut me off while I was driving or he pulled his car in so closely to mine, in a parking space, that I couldn't open my door. Finally, though he had driven a couple of different cars and a truck, I realized it was the same guy. He was obviously following me. And, who knows how long he had been doing this for? Ultimately, he was doing this in order to create a fight.

Realizing his nonsense, during one situation, I pulled out my camera phone, took his picture, took a photograph of his car and his license plate, and proceeded to call the police on my cell phone. I told him who I was calling and that I was going to get a restraining order against him. He yelled a few, *"Fuck you's,"* and went away. I guess due to the photos I had, he stayed away. I mean what would fighting a loser like that prove anyway?

Which leads me to a realization that was provided to me a few years before this incident that involved me being stalked. I was out one night, and this one guy made my life-situation very clear. This is also one of the main reasons I do not tweet.

In any case... I had mentioned on my website where I was going to be one night. When my friend and I showed up there, I noticed one guy giving me a hard-stare from across the room. I didn't think that much about it. Then, when we moved onto a different place, and I saw him again, I took notice. In any case, this guy knew who I was, came up and begin making some snide comments. He kept trying to get me exasperated enough so he could start a fight with me. (And fighting, is just stupid. It is the lowest level of human existence). None-the-less, when he finally said one thing to much, I was about to end the conversation with my fist. Luckily, before I did, he said, *"I know you're probably going to win this fight, but when you do I'm going to call the police, have you arrested, then I'm going to sue you, because you're Scott Shaw, 8th degree black belt."* I laughed. I walked away. It made me realize that I can never get in a fight, because of who and what I am. If I were to get in a fight, they would have me arrested and would sue me. Even if they say they won't; they will... I know, because a friend of mine, who is in a similar situation to me, went through a similar experience and didn't hold back his fists; he got arrested, convicted, and sued all because of who he was and what he accomplished.

Now, I'm not even going to talk about the people who come up to me at cafes or restaurants that I frequent, time and time again, asking me to read their script or finance their movie. Because, I don't do either, I just simply guide them on their way or stop going to the establishment. But, dudes, when I say, *"No,"* once, that should be enough. Stop stalking me!

Then, there are the Internet stalkers. Oh my god... What a bunch of losers... They criticize any movie or any book I put out. Some of them due to so subtlety, it is like poetry. In fact, there was this one university employed Ph.D. who used to go after me restlessly. I never understood why. He never met me. He didn't know me. But, he would constantly rip on me every chance he got.

The fact of the matter is, all he ever did, by behaving like that, was to make himself look bad; especially when he did stuff hiding behind, *"Anonymous,"* on one site but then use his name, while stating the same thing, in the exact same words, on another site.

And, this is something that other Internet stalkers need to keep in mind. Ultimately, you just make yourself look bad.

In fact, I would bet, that most of these people, who go after my stuff, have never seen the films they are criticizing or read the books they are critiquing. They certainly don't know me. They just want to throw a cheap shot at me. Some of them go on and on everyplace they can find a spot to spew their nonsense about my creations, my philosophies, and me.

The funny thing about this, I find amusing. It is kind of like Andy Warhol... He didn't care what the critics said. All he would do was to measure the amount of type space they gave him.

Any publicity is good publicity... Every time somebody criticizes a movie or a book, it makes people curious; it just makes it sell more copies.

But, there is a really important fact that stalkers need to realize. The reason they never accomplish what they really want to do with their life is because, they are wasting all of their time focusing on the lives of others. They waste their life-time doing all that kind of nonsense.

Speaking of that, I remember when my first book on Hapkido was published. Some studio owner, from the South, I forget his name, sent me email-after-email, as he was all up in arms about the fact that I wore stripes on my belt in the photographs in the book and he believed this to be totally, *"Un-Hapkido."* I was much more forgiving back then. So, to stop all of his nonsense, I finally answered his email. He then sent me a photograph from a 1960s black belt magazine showing how the Hapkido instructor in it didn't wear strips on his belt. The funny thing about all this was, the guy in the picture was one of my first instructors and I was there when the photographs were taken at the studio. This combined with the fact that the guy criticized me as being, *"Too Taekwondo."* I mean, come on, I am every bit as Taekwondo as I am Hapkido. I have been involved in both for virtually all of my life and everybody knows that...

The guy also went on about how he hated the book, and so on. What he and many other people do not realize is, when a respected international publisher, like the publisher of that book, asks you to write a book about a subject, they give you an outline of what they want you to write about, how many words the manuscript will be, and how many photographs you will provide them with. So, as with many of my other books, published by respected publishers, you give them what they ask for, then their editors have at it. FYI people, the author, in actuality, has very little control!

Finally, I got the guy to end our discourse by my suggesting to him that if he didn't like the book, he should write one of his own, and get it published. *"I will! Oh, I will!"* Of course, nothing ever came of this. He never had a book published.

Again, this just goes back to people wasting their life-time focusing on the lives and the works of others.

People who are accomplished do not do this. They do not behave in this manner or fashion. They do not stalk people either in life or on the Internet. Why? Because they are too busy creating their own legacy, instead of trying to get their fifteen minutes of fame by critiquing the works of others. Or, by trying to mess with somebody else's life...

Get a life people !!!

What Are You Thinking?

What are you thinking? Few people spend any time considering this. They simply pass through their life, allowing their mind to roam wherever it will, being control by whatever emotion or desire comes into play. It is for this reason that those on the spiritual path decide to meditate to find out the source of their thoughts. From this, they come to a unique understanding of SELF and why they do what they do—why they think what they think.

The spiritual path is not easy. Letting your mind run ramped, that is easy. It takes no control. But, what happens from this lack of control is a wasted life, with no focus or accomplishment.

Every person who has ever achieved anything has done so through a precise sense of focus. And, this has nothing to do with spirituality. It has to do with mental focus. So, if you do not choose to consider yourself spiritual, if you do not choose to walk the spiritual path, this does not mean that a focused mind will not help you.

In Zen and Yoga, the practitioner is trained to silence the mind through meditation. With a silenced mind, very clear perception of life is gained. This is because of the fact that, as your thoughts are turned off, when you emerge from meditation, you see life from a very NEW and clear perspective.

Though meditation is great tool for silencing the mind and perhaps coming into contact with the divine self, unless it is taken to the next step, it does not reveal the source of your thoughts and why you think what you think. Psychotherapy is a great tool for this, but that requires another person, (a therapist's), interaction.

To get to the source of what you think and why you are thinking it on your own, all you must do is dive deep into your own mind. Start by observing what you are thinking right now. Ask yourself, *"Why am I thinking that?"* Once you have an answer, go deeper and question, *"What made me think that way?"* Continue back further and further until you find the source of your thoughts.

This technique is not easy, nor is it for everyone. It takes a desire for mental focus and understanding YOUR SELF. It is for those who want to focus their lives to the degree that they can succeed at what every undertaking they are desirous of, while truly coming to an exacting sense of SELF. From this, life is not wasted pursuing meaningless activities that may eventually come back to haunt and hinder your life.

Consciously Doing or Doing Consciously

We all have things we have to do in life. Some we like. Some we do not. Some we used to like and no longer like. Some we previously didn't like and now we do.

There is laundry to do, trash to take out, lawns to be mowed, dishes to be done, clothing to be hung up, etc. Some people like to do things that we hate. While we love to do things that others hate. This is all based in personality.

From a spiritual perspective, it is taught that we must accept what don't like and do it anyway. By interacting with life in this fashion we remove resistance from our lives. This allows us to see the necessity of action. From this, ultimately, we will join into the universal perfection.

Tell yourself that when you are in a traffic jam and are late for a meeting…

In Zen, they actually have people do things that are very abstract. Things that most people would never want to do. And, the doing of these things is, often times, not comfortable at all.

For example, take two steps, go down on your knees, bow to the ground, get up, and take two more.

The average person would say, *"That's stupid. Why bother?"* Whereas the person walking the spiritual path understands that this is a form of meditation—that doing this type of practice, focuses the mind to the degree where preforming the average actions of life, no matter how menial, becomes more conscious and, in fact, its own form of meditation.

So, here is the choice. And, it is a choice. You can do what you're doing, while you love it or hate it. Or, you can do what you're doing and see it as a meditation leading to a higher consciousness.

But, you have to keep in mind, the fact of the matter is, these are both just Mind-Stuff. You are telling yourself to feel a certain way, while you pretend to be giving yourself an enhanced reason to do what you do.

This is the subtle ploy of the spiritual lifestyle and the reason people walking the spiritual path appear to be more fulfilled. They know, (they have practiced), how to better lie to themselves about their Life-Stuff.

Like I say, over-and-over, it is your life, you can make your choices.

Zen and the Void

A few days ago, I was discussing the fact that the world of music is changing. It has gone from vinyl LPs to CD, and now simply to sound files kept on a flash drive or hard drive. With this evolution something is lost. The physical presence is gone, leaving only the abstract and the nondescript.

From a spiritual perspective, this appears to parallel the path of advancing human conscious. As one merges with the ultimate mind, enlightenment, they go from something to nothing, from formed reality into the abstract void.

The void is this strange abstract place; undefinable. Known but unknown.

The process of music production and its archiving has, in many ways, come full circle. It has gone from a place where people played music, but there was no way to harness it or record it and keep what a person personally played for posterity as there was no way to record it.

Like satori, it was in a place known only to itself. Only experienced for the moment it was lived.

If a tree falls in the forest and no one is there to hear it, does it make a sound at all?

In the space of a century or so, music went from a place of not being able to be physically recorded, to being captured in order that it may be heard at a later time. In this process, it has gone through a few different physical formats, until it has again reached this abstract phase, where it is today. A place where, if you didn't know what a hard drive or flash drive was, if you don't know the operating system or the program, the music has once again entered into the zero of only an abstract object possessing something, yet nothing.

Is this the paradox of evolving human consciousness or simply an easier way to erase the legacy of what each person contributes? In either case, it goes back to the ultimate spiritual perspective, *"Life means nothing."* The only thing that means anything is the value that man (or woman) and their egos place upon it. When the person is gone, when their ego is gone, either through enlightenment or death, the mind enters the perfect space of emptiness, of void.

____The World Didn't End! Again...

Last Saturday, May 21, once again, the world was predicted to end by some fanatic religious group and its teacher. Obviously, it did not. Surprise!

The guy who made this prediction and the church he represents is worth an estimate one hundred and twenty-million dollars. All of this money came to them from donations. Just like all the money that goes into the Catholic Church.

To the Catholic Church, these donations financed pedophiles and paying off those who were abused by the pedophiles. To this guy and his group, they spent a lot of their money on billboards, newspaper advertisements, and other methods, predicating the end of the world.

Wake up people! Who are you giving your money to?

In my lifetime, this was not the first time the world was supposed to end. The first I heard of this exact-date Armageddon nonsense was when I was in sixth grade. My best friend's mother was a Jehovah Witness. They had it down to a science that the world was to end in 1974 and only the holy would ascend to heaven. Back then; I had it calculated that hopefully I would get my driver's license before it happened. As driving, of course, is a big desire in a younger's life.

It never happened. Wow, surprise...

Sadly, my friend, due to his mother's religion and it never letting him do anything like, join the boy scouts, or have Christmas, went down the wrong road. He got arrested a lot of times in junior high and the last time I ran into him was when I was in tenth grade; he had dropped out and soon after was sent up for a long stint at a juvenile prison facility.

Though there were a few other minor end-of-the-world predictions, the next big one came at the transition of the twentieth to the twenty-first century. All hell was promised to break loose. Only the holy would survive and ascend to heaven.

Heaven, oh yeah, that's where I want to be; with a bunch of hypocritical, judgmental, superstitious people.

In any case, nothing happened. Though I did have a friend or two that made all kinds of plans in preparation.

Prior to my life, I heard a report that in 1840 was probably the biggest congregation for assentation of those awaiting the rapture in U.S. history. People gave up all that they own, put on white clothing, headed up to the hills, and waited for the return of Jesus. He never came.

It is hard to not wonder what these people do once they have given up everything—probably given it to their church, and then must go on with their lives. They must start over. And, whom can they believe? Certainly not the prophets of doom that guided them down the road to absolutely nothing.

It is also hard not to wonder why people choose to believe this style of apocalyptic nonsense. Is their life so empty and the superstition so strong that they need to hold onto, to believe something/anything, even though all logic has time-and-time again proven it to be nonessential? I don't know... But these predications and the amount of people that believe in them always amaze me.

The Dojang Experience

The Korean term, *"Dojang,"* is used to describe a martial art training facility. The Japanese term, *"Dojo,"* is perhaps the more commonly known word, used to describe the same training space.

Most people have the belief that a dojang is some sort of scared space where only the higher learning of the martial arts is transacted. For me, this was, amusingly, not the case.

My first martial art training began when I was six. Though, in fact, I had always possessed a rudimentary understanding of the martial and fighting arts as my father earned his black belt during World War II and my uncle had been a professional boxer prior to World War II.

My first teacher was a Korean born Hapkido black belt. This man was probably one of the first Hapkido black belts to immigrate to the U.S. Though he never owned a formal school, he was one of the first people, I know of, to have taught Hapkido in the U.S.; though he referred to it by one of its earlier names, Ho Shin Moo Do. Me, as a six-year-old, I just thought I was studying Karate.

This man made his living as a gardener, and he trained a group of young South Korean student in his back yard. As he was a friend of my father's, I was allowed to train with them.

I always remember how nicely groomed his yard was. He had a couple of nicely trimmed trees, and nice flowers and plants lined his fence. I mean, he was a gardener after all...

The man would train the five or six of us, as he walked around with a bamboo staff to smack us with, if we did something wrong, and a cigarette hanging out of his mouth. I didn't really think that much about it as both of my parents smoked. In fact, even my dentist, who was also Asian, used to sit overlooking his dentist chair, with a cigarette burning behind him, as he examined my teeth. It was obviously a different era. ☺

After earning my black belt, I eventually went to a couple different dojangs through my teenage years, as we moved around the L.A. area more than a little bit. All were operated by Korean born teachers. And, though they didn't walk around the training floor smoking as they taught their classes, they all would sit at their desk or in their waiting room, smoking.

By the time I was twenty-one, I was helping a newly arrived Korean master I had met in Seoul establish his business. I taught virtually all of his classes for him for years. Though he had a No Smoking sign behind his desk, he constantly smoked in the dojang. Perhaps even more interesting is the fact that each day he would have his friends come by and they would go out to the central dojang floor, sit there smoking, drinking, and playing Ma Jak. Ma Jak is more commonly known as Mahjong. It is a Korean gambling game that they would play all day.

If you have ever watched Koreans playing this game, it is quite a site. They get all excited as they yell and scream as they toss down the small tiles, (which are kind of like dominos), and are used to win or lose the game.

He was actually one of my two most influential teachers. He was already in forties but was still a great physical technician. For those non-martial artists out there, who may not be aware of this, by the time you reach your forties, having practiced the martial arts for your entire life, your body is most commonly rapidly breaking down, maybe even already trashed, due to all of the harsh training that goes hand-in-hand with the martial arts. But, he could still fly through the air quite gracefully.

We became good friends. He and I would go out and get drunk at the Korean hostess bars in Koreatown, at strips clubs, and occasionally partake of other substances. But, those are other stories…

One thing that most people probably don't understand is that, even though most South Korean men are avid churchgoers, they are very old school. They, like I, judge a man by how much he can drink. Though I was only twenty-one when I first began working with this man, I had already, long ago, developed the ability to be able to drink round-for-round with the best of 'em. So, I was readily accepted into their community. Few non-Koreans are ever let inside this world.

Eventually, he got remarried, stopped the partying, and several years later, he and I had a major falling out. I never saw him again. But, that's fine, *"Falling out,"* lets you move away from one situation and chart out new territories.

But, I always fondly remember his school and how for the years I worked with him, he and his friends would sit around the training floor, smoking and play Ma Jak each days as they yelled while they threw down the tile pieces and screamed at each other.

Dojangs are not always what they seem. ☺

The Spirituality of Doing

There has always been this belief that the truly spiritual are somehow, someway not supposed to do anything. By some magical method they are supposed to have all of the money they need, supplied by god, or whomever, and they are supposed to exist on this plane of reality that few others can even comprehend. But, the reality of spirituality is not like that.

When I was young devotee of Swami Satchidananda, he had a home in the hills of Montecito, California. He drove a totally resorted vintage 1958 Cadillac. A bit strange for a guru, even I thought. But, that was what he did.

One day I was at his home, and he was discussing with a few of the other disciple around him how the radio had gone out in his car. He drove it to the shop and the guy was going to charge him an additional $100.00 if he had to take it out for him to investigate what was wrong. So, he decided to go home, take it out himself, and bring it back to the guy, saving himself $100.00. That was pretty logical, I surmised. But, everyone around him was flabbergasted that our guru would be getting his hands dirty and doing menial labor.

But, what is true spirituality? Isn't it living life? Isn't it doing life things?

I think a lot of pretend gurus that rose out of the 1960s counterculture consciousness propagated the fact that they were simply supposed to be taken care of, do nothing, just be given money, title and whatever. They were too good to do anything, as they were so enlightened. The problem is, this is the understanding that has spread out through modern society. It has defined the spiritual. But, it is not real. It is only pretense and pretend.

A truly spiritual; a truly enlightened person does whatever life-action they need to do. That is the true essence of spirituality; not expecting but doing. Like the old Zen proverb states, *"Before enlightenment chop wood, carry water. After enlightenment chop wood, carry water."*

_____Justice

If I haven't made it to the gym when the evening rolls around, sometimes I take a walk around my neighborhood to get my heart rate up and my blood flowing. Last night as I was leaving for a walk, (a power-walk if you will), I walked by my car which I had left parked on the street. There were a few neighborhood kids standing around it as they shot off these toy guns. There was a drink sitting on my trunk. As I walked up, one of the kids grabbed it. I nicely said, *"Hey dudes, that's my car, please don't put anything on it."* The kid with the drink in his hand said, *"I didn't..." "I just saw you!"*

I smiled... His answer was so descriptive of life.

Do you ever notice when you watch shows like Cops or when people get caught doing something that they're not supposed to do, they always say, *"I didn't do it."* It's kind of like life, we all know what's right and what's wrong but sometimes we do what's wrong anyway. But, we don't want to get caught. If we do, all that happens is lies...

There's also the other side of the issue...

One of my earliest memories was when my father beat the crap out of me for doing something he thought I did, when, in fact, I didn't do it at all. I was five.

That was back in the day when parents would smack their kids whenever they did something they didn't like. Now, they would probably get arrested for child abuse. But, that was a different time.

As the story goes, my father opened a very successful bar and restaurant near the U.S.C.

campus back in the early 1950s. He named it the Trojan Barrel. He ran it until he sold it in the mid 1960s to move onto, what he believed to be, the bigger and the better... As U.S.C. is located in Southcentral L.A., the area was and is predominately made up of African-Americans. As this was back in the early 1960s, like many businesses, houses flanked my father's restaurant. So, I used to play with the next-door neighbor kids. In fact, when I was five, I received my first kiss on the lips from the sweet little African-American girl who lived next-door.

One evening, the cook for my father's restaurant, Calvin, brought his son by. His name was Junior. Probably it was actually Calvin Jr. but he went by Junior. I took him to meet my friends. The next-door neighbor kids all thought his name was very funny. They keep going on and on about, *"Junior, Junior, Junior."* I knew this was wrong and said absolutely nothing. He ran in crying to his father. My father grabbed me by the arm, and though I kept telling him I didn't say anything, he pulled off his belt and beat my bottom. There and then I understood; in life, truth didn't matter and there was no true justice.

So, here is the life-dilemma, like I have long discussed, *"Everybody lies..."* So, we each come to expect it when something goes wrong. That person must be lying, right? But, are they? And, how do you believe them?

Many would discuss the concept of trust. But, trust doesn't equal truth. It only equals trust. And, many times, as has been proven, people lie to those who trust them.

The other side of the issue is that people lie to set up other people—to make them fall for the deeds they, themselves, actually committed.

In addition, how many times have people believed something, based on whatever fabrication of reality was told to them, and then tried to make others conform to it even if their compliance was based upon another person's, a political system's, an overseeing governing body's, or a religion's lies?

The only ultimate truth is, spoken truth cannot be the defining factor for anything. Because, if it is judged by others as being truth or falsehood, then egos and desires come into play.

What does this mean? Don't believe in truth, it does not exist. All that exists is this place we call, *"Life."* And, LIFE is riddle with the untruthful.

What we do in LIFE is up to us. The repercussions or the karma we encounter is all set in motion by who we hang out with, what we do, and how we do it.

It's your life choice. You get to make it...

Do Your Business

I recently took a watch to this guy in Belmont Shores to be cleaned. His shop had been around for thirty years, so he seemed like a safe enough place to drop it off.

He called me the next day, gave me the estimate, and told it would take one to two weeks to complete. It all sounded fine.

Two weeks in, I hadn't heard from him, so I called him. He told me he had to order a part. The part would be in on Wednesday, and he should have it done in another week; call him then. This I did.

"Hi, I'm checking on my watch..."
"Oh, I have to order a part for it. It's going to come in next week."
"That's what you told me last week."

He choked up for a moment.

"They sent me the wrong part. But, it will be done by Tuesday."

Though I did not believe his initial answer. Whatever... I let it go and I went in the shop on the following Tuesday. The lady behind the counter had no idea about when the watch would be done. She opened a drawer and saw that there were literally hundreds of unfinished watches in there.

"He's not in right now. He'll be back later..."

I began to see the game. It is just like my friend who has been making, customizing, and repairing my guitars for thirty years. A great guy! But, he is so overwhelmed, nothing ever gets done, and he hopes people will just forget about the guitar or amp they left. Some of my guitars have sat in his stacks for literally a decade or more. In fact, every now and then he finds one that I gave him some time back in the '80s and we had both totally forgotten about.

He's my friend, the watch repair guy isn't. I kept calling.

Finally, due to my not letting up, he got the job done; a little over six weeks in.

Here's the reality... Had he told me it was going to take six weeks, that would have been fine. Just tell me. He wouldn't have heard from me for six weeks. But, don't tell me one or two weeks and then get pissy at me when I'm calling to find out about the status.

This is good lesson to learn in life for all of us. First of all, people promise you things so they can take your money. Be careful whom you believe. Secondarily, don't promise what you can't do. Be real. It just makes all of life simpler and a lot less emotionally complicated.

At the end of the day, this guy lost other business, as I had a couple of other watches that needed cleaning and repair. Had he been straight, he would have got the job. Now, the job goes elsewhere...

_____You Ruined My Life!

Life is lived by a series of interrelationships. Some of these relationships last for days, weeks, months, even years, while others only exist within the moment of a glance. Many people define their lives by their relationships—both in a positive and a negative fashion. Some people are very proud of the people they know, while others feel someone else has negatively altered their life or has hurt them.

How many times have we each heard, *"You broke my heart." "That person took all my money."* Or, *"You introduced me to that person and they ruined my life."* And, these are just a few of the examples. We have each heard our own set of life defining statements, discussing a person who someone believes truly hurt them.

In life, the reality is, there are positive and there are negative people. We each meet those from both of these group as we transverse our paths.

Some people are intentionally negative—they consciously do bad things; knowing what they are doing is not right. But, most people aren't like that, however. Though they may do something that you do not like, they did not do it with mal-intent. They simply did what felt right to them. And, this is the kicker; people do what feels right to them.

For example, if you don't love a person, you shouldn't stay with them. But, tell that to the person on the other end of the relationship that is totally smitten. You leave, you break their heart, and they hate your forever. Or, if you tell a person about the path you are following and they try it out and it doesn't work for them, they blame you for all of the time and money they wasted. Again, these are just a couple of examples. But, the reality is, people want someone to blame. They want a cause for their misfortune or unhappiness. They do not want to own or take responsibility for their choices and particularly their desires that lead them to their choices. As such, they focus all this ill-will and negative energy towards someone they feel wronged them, but they never look at how they may have wronged the other person in the process of that particular life-relationship.

Perhaps a person wasn't happy in a relationship and left it. What did their life loose from all of the time that they remained in it when they knew they should go? And, what did it cost them? Often times money, new opportunities, and the ability to move forward in the life-direction that they hoped. Perhaps a life-changing opportunity was lost due to the simple fact of remaining in a relationship longer than they should have. And, this concept does not simply define personal relationships; it also goes on to business and other types of relationships, as well. But, the person on the other side/the blaming side, never thinks about or realizes this. All they know is that their heart, was broken, their life was altered when the person left. So, they seek revenge. This may occur in terms of words or physical actions. But, in either case, it does not change the reality that each person must be allowed to live out their choices and move in the direction they feel is best for them.

The fact of the matter is, we all must deal with people in our lives. Hopefully, we are able to surround ourselves with those of a positive nature—those that can nurture the relationship and positive gains can be made from the two life's interacting. Hopefully, but that is not always the case.

Life is based upon personal choice. Personal choice equals what one person wants and the other person doesn't.

So, you can blame. You can scream, *"You ruined my life!"* Or, you can see the dissolving of each relationship was a positive motivator for change. And, change is good. It keeps life interesting...

_____In the Waning Days of Vinyl

In the waning days of vinyl there used to be some great boutique record stores here in L.A. and in some of my other haunts like San Francisco, Santa Cruz, and London. You could go in and find some really unique and often times great music, housed in really artistic record jackets. And, you'd only pay like $1.00 for them.

It was really an experience because you would never know what you might find. Then came CDs...

One of the biggest complains about CD, when they rose to prominence, was the fact that they were so small. As such, the artwork was so much smaller. And, though I heartily embraced this new format, I agreed; looking at the art and/or the photographs on a CD was not the same as looking at it on a full-sized LP.

What also quickly occurred, with the dawning of CDs, is that no longer was vinyl just vinyl; now it had become collectable. So, the prices went up and up and up in the record stores. No longer could you go into a store and find a really unique collection of music for one or two dollars. Now, it was ten or twenty...

What I quickly realized with the dawning of the CD age was that a lot of great music was going to be lost. As there wasn't enough of a market for some of the artists, their albums would cease to be produced and the music that they create would be forgotten. In many cases, this has come to pass.

As time went on, and the economy went downhill, virtually all of the aforementioned record stores went out of business. Now, the only place to find vinyl is on the Internet or in a Thrift Store. The problem with the Internet is you have to know what you are looking for. The problem with Thrift Stores is nothing is organized; it is all just a mess, so it takes a long time to look through it. And, many times the record is just totally trashed if you actually find something.

Recently, I have noticed that large collections of CDs are showing up in Thrift Stores. As the digital age had taken hold, it is obvious that many people are trashing their CDs the same way they did with their vinyl twenty-five years ago. Though this has brought a lot of cool CDs into play, there is a big problem. This is the end of an era.

In fact, I know this one girl who, last year, put all of her CD collection on an external hard drive and then went around to the homes of everyone she knew and digitally acquired every CD each person had onto that same hard drive. Then, she trashed all of her CDs. Yes, she now has a great collection of music. But, operating systems change and hard drives crash; losing all that is on them. So, though this is the next wave, it is not a great way to archive music.

With the replacing of CDs for vinyl, there was still a physical object to be had. But, with the replacing of CDs for hard drive memory space, at the end of the day there will nothing. There will be no cool vinyl or even CD to find somewhere. There will be no going into a boutique music store and discovering that very cool band just by being attracted to the artwork on the album cover. To quote the great Bob Dylan, *"The times they are a changin'."* To quote me, *"Change isn't always for the better..."*

___Gentlemen Remove Their Hats

Ever since I was a young boy, I was taught that when a man, (when a gentleman), enters a building, if they are wearing a hat, they take it off. This tradition can certainly be seen in the movies from the 1930s and 1940s when virtually every man wore a fedora.

Yesterday morning I was doing one of those Sunday brunch things at a rather high-end restaurant. In comes a young couple with their baby and they were sat down next to us. The man, worn a very junky looking John Deere baseball style cap. It really stuck me that he did not even think about removing it. And, this is not just him... Though the primary hat style has changed from fedora to baseball caps, men never seem to take off their hats when they enter a building anymore. I mean do they have absolutely no class? Did their parents not teach them anything? Did they not choose to learn what is right and what is wrong?

I remember maybe a decade back when this one friend of mine and myself when to have an expensive smoke, over cocktails, at a cigar bar that was owned and operated by the actor George Hamilton in Beverly Hills. My friend was sprouting a black fedora. The moment he walked into the establishment, and he did not take off his hat, the barkeep asked him to, *"Please remove your hat."* Which I think was totally appropriate. But, nobody does that anymore. Nobody says anything and nobody knows or cares enough to understand that wearing a hat indoor is not appropriate.

I certainly understand that times changes. But, baseball hats, though obviously a great tool for sun protection, just do not look good. They certainly do not look good in restaurants. And, people don't even realize how foolish they look providing the free advertising space for whatever company the hat details.

Dudes, when you go inside, take off your hats!

Migraine

I was watching the news last night and this one field reporter came on. I remember how a few months ago she had an onscreen meltdown. She was talking and all that came out was gibberish. I thought I knew what might be happening to her, but it wasn't until, instead of reporting a story, she became the story a few days later. Her doctors had concluded that she didn't have a stroke as was initially thought, but instead, had experienced a migraine.

Yes, migraines can do that to you. They can leave you with the inability to speak. I know, because it has happened to me.

I first experienced a migraine, specifically an ocular migraine, when I was fourteen years old. It occurred one day during high school. This type of migraine affects your vision. What happens is that it is like a camera flash has gone off in your eyes. There are all these swirling colors in your central vision and all you are left with is your peripheral vision. The first time I experienced an ocular migraine, it last for three days.

As I grew up in a very emotionally repressive household, it was all about the, *"Do not feel."* And, as I had already developed the, *"Just tough it out,"* mentality by that point in my life, I told no one. I had no idea what it was. But, as you can image, it was pretty scary.

These ocular migraines continued periodically throughout my teens. Thankfully, none lasted as long as my first one. But, sometimes they would last all day.

I never told anybody about them. I just kept the experiences to myself. But, I obviously did think something very bad was going wrong with me.

As time went on, they got worse. The first time I had a similar experience to the one encountered by the reporter was when I was traveling in Oregon. My girlfriend, (at the time), and I had been to Canada; specifically, Vancouver Island. We had returned to go to the Rainbow Festival that was to be held, that year, in the mountains of Oregon. This was a gathering where hippies and holies would congregate for a week in the summer each year. Though the location was highly guarded and very difficult to find, we arrived via the muddy Oregon mountain roads, as it had been raining the night before.

I parked, we packed up our necessary items: sleeping bags, a tent, and the like, and began our trek in. The trail was very muddy and very slippery. An ocular migraine kicked in on me. It was very hard to keep my footing as I could barely see the trail in front of me.

As we walked further in, the vision problems continued, and I got the pounding headache and the nausea that came hand-in-hand with the altered vision. Finally, we got to the valley where the festival was being held. By then, I couldn't speak. Though my mind could clearly articulate every thought, if I tried to say something, nothing coherent came out, only words that I didn't mean to say.

The conditions at the festival were horrible. Between the mud, the way too many hippies, and the generalized bad/dirty conditions of the site, I did not want to stay. As I couldn't really verbally communicate, I set up the tent, and I rested for some time. I guess my girlfriend was unaware of what was going on with me. She probably thought I was having some sort of spiritual experience. When I could finally get words out, I said, *"Let's go."* With this, we packed up the tent, walked back up the muddy trail, got in my van, and drove off.

The next time this type of intense migraine occurred to me was a few months later. My friend and I were riding our motorcycles up to the top of Mount Wilson. This is a mountain that overlooks Los Angeles. On the way up, I began to develop an ocular migraine. We were driving on a twisty mountain road that is flanked on one side by a massive cliff. Very scary!

By the time we got to the top, I couldn't speak. Again, the thoughts were very clear in my mind, but I couldn't articulate anything. After we looked out over the smoggy city for a few minutes, all I could do was pull all of my mental focus together and spit out the word, *"Well..."* We started our bikes and drove down the mountain.

I truly gave into the fact that I was going to die on the journey down the mountain that day. I was riding a motorcycle. All I had was peripheral vision. My central vision was blocked with flashy, spinning lights, *"Crystal vision,"* as I came to call it. I couldn't speak. And, there were numerous boulders, of various sizes, on the road that had fallen down the night before and had not yet been swept off and over the cliff by the rangers that had a specially designed truck to do just that. I knew I was dead. But miraculously, I made it down the mountain and made it home. I waved at my friend when we got to my street. I went home, thinking/knowing something very-very-very bad was happening to me.

One of the big problems about migraines is that you never know when they will occur. As I didn't really know what was happening to me or what it actually meant, I became very concerned, even paranoid, about when the next one would take place. It really ruined a lot of my fun during that period of my life.

It wasn't until a few years later, when I was in a college general ed. health class, that I actually learned what was happening to me. We were studying headaches and the professor began to describe her experiences with migraines. She described her symptoms, and they were exactly the same as mine. I wasn't the only one. Nor was the reporter.

I think many people are like me, they just keep these things to themselves and never known, until they know. So, for those of you who didn't know, now I trust you do... I hope this helps. You're not alone.

_____Got Any Change?

      I had breakfast this morning at one of my usual haunts. I ordered a vegetarian burrito and asked them to hold the weird garden burger junk they normally include. I just stuck with the brown rice and veggies. I read the *L.A. Weekly* and it was all-good. I finished. The server gave me my check. I paid with a twenty-dollar bill and she returned with the change. She gave me a five-dollar bill, a one-dollar bill, and two quarters. Now here's was my dilemma. My bill was about $13.00. Normally for a bill like that I would leave a $2.00 or $3.00 tip. But, she only gave me a five and a one. I checked but the only other bills I had were large. So, no help.

      The question? Did she do this so she would get a big tip? Or, was she willing to settle for a $1.50.

      I smiled. I like her. She delivered the food to my table more than a few times over the past few years and she seems very nice. I left her the five-spot. ☺

Lemon Ice Cubes

People are always questioning what they can do to make their life just a little bit better. Have you ever squeezed or juiced lemons and put them in an ice cube tray. Then, the next time you have a glass of wine, a beer, some tea, or a soft drink put the lemon ice cubes in your glass. Not only does this process add a unique flavor to the drink but it makes it more fun, as well. You get to drink some lemon pulp.

If you want to change your living environment and don't want to spend too much money, change the plates around your electrical sockets and your light switches. There are some really cool plates out there now. Some are simple and some are more elaborate but even if you just change the color of your electrical switch plate it can completely change the look of your dwellings and make your walls a little bit more fun to look at.

Change is easy and it doesn't have to be expensive. Making your life just a little bit better is easy to accomplish.

Fantasy

Each of us has fantasies. We travel into our minds and live out all kinds of events with people and with situations that we wish would happen. Some say that when you fantasize, in some ways on some plane, you are actually living what you are fantasizing about. But, let's think about this for a moment...

A couple of amusing examples, from my life experiences, come to mind. One of them is, my bud Venchinzo and I were kickin' it at *The Rainbow* one night. In the dimly lighted dance floor I met this Japanese girl who I thought was just stunning. It was already late in the evening when our paths crossed and the friend she was with was tired, so she was going to leave. We set a meet for the next day at *Farmer's Market.* As you can image, that night my mind continually went to her and what may come from our meeting the next day.

The next day arrives, I show up at *Farmer's Market,* and there she was. From a distance, she was every bit the beauty that I thought her to be. I sat down and we began to talk. She opened her mouth and, oh my god! She obviously never brushed her teeth. I mean never! They were really scary...

Now, I don't mean to be stereotypical here, but as someone who has lived and spent a lot of time in Japan, I can tell you with certainty, unlike the West, the Japanese are not that much into dental hygiene. This girl was the perfect example. I could hardly even look at her, as her teeth were so bad.

Another time I remember was when I was living in Shanghai. I had met this girl a few days before and we had set a date to meet. I anxiously awaited our meeting, full of all the hope and fantasies that can be expected from a young man in his twenties. On the night of our date, we hooked up and we were walking down the street. Though she was a very beautiful and seemingly stylish woman, she stopped as we walked and let loose with a major spit right on the street. Certainly, this was a cultural thing. But... It certainly killed any fantasy I had about her.

This is the point. Fantasies are the perfect situation created in your mind. The people, the places, and the actions all live out perfectly. In life, however, things are not that way. People are people and life is life. So, for those who say that on a certain level when you are fantasizing you are actually living the experience, they are wrong. You are not. All you are living is your mind's perfect projection of how you hope people, places, and events will be lived out. As you do not or cannot know the person fully: who they are, or how they will react; just as you cannot define how any event will be lived in your life, due to the millions of circumstances that surround and define it; all a fantasy is—is a fantasy. It is all in your mind. Don't mistake it for something else.

_____Stop Blaming Others
for the Mistakes You Make!

People should really stop blaming other for the mistakes that they, themselves, make. I mean it is such a common occurrence that people say, *"You told me I should do that."* Or, *"You introduced me to that person and they turned out to be a real asshole."*

Instead of blaming somebody else, you made the choice, now own it!

The fact of the matter is, we have all done things that we wish we didn't do. This fact is simply one of the realities of life. We can either live with our choices, learn from them, and move on. Or, we let any negative outcome become the defining factor of our life. Which do you think is a better end result?

I remember the first time somebody blamed me for their choice. My friend, who was a couple of years older than me, had moved to the valley to go to college. He lived in one of the dorms. I was still in Hollywood, going to Hollywood High School. This was back in the seventies when we were all still eating a lot of Acid and doing other mind-altering drugs. Anyway, this one guy who lived in the dorms with my friend really wanted to try Acid. As he had no access to it, and knowing I lived in Hollywood, he kept asking me and asking me to, *"Please,"* get him some. Finally, I gave in to his requests and brought him a hit of blotter.

Now, LSD can be very scary, and I do not recommend it for anyone. It can especially be scary the first time you take it. This was obviously the case with this guy. A week or so later, and from that point forward, all I heard from this guy was, *"Why'd you buy it for me? Why'd you give it to me?"* Etcetera, etcetera... *"Why? Because you kept begging me to get it for you!"*

In more recent times a guy I know was considering buying a house in the South Bay area of L.A. where I have lived pretty much since I graduate college. Now, this area is not for everyone. It is a bit removed from the city. This is why when the guy asked me if he should buy this one particular house, overlooking the ocean, I did not answer his questions. It is just one of those things that you cannot tell a person, where they should live. Then, the minute he bought the house, I began getting calls, *"Why didn't you tell me it was so far. It takes me like forty minutes or an hour to even get to my old house to load up my car with stuff to try to move it. And, now I am so far from my acting classes..."*

In this case, I didn't even say anything. But, he blamed me none-the-less.

I am sure, in each of our lives, we have similar experiences where someone has either asked us to do something for them or asked us our opinion and our response guided them in an undesired direction.

This is life. We all make mistakes. We all do things that we wish we hadn't done.

But, what is a mistake? Isn't it simply our interpretation of a specific set of events? And, what defines a mistake? What we like or dislike.

So how we define a mistake, what constitutes a mistake, is simply defined by us.

We can make each experience a learning experience or we can see it as a mistake. It is up to you how you define your life events. So, stop blaming others for the mistakes you make.

Howl

I was watching the movie, *Howl,* starring James Franco last night. The movie is, of course, about Allen Ginsberg. Perhaps it is not a great and all-telling portrayal of his life, but it is, none-the-less, a good film.

I was watching the movie with a woman who is a decade or so younger than me and one of the main things I noticed is how many of the idioms in the written words of Ginsberg went right by her. She is too young to have ever heard them and she did not know or care to know what the words actually meant. I think this is the case with pretty much every generation. How, what we say, how we speak, and the slang that we use is only truly understood and embraced by a specific group of people, at a specific point in history. Then, though someone may look up a word or a term in some slang dictionary, the true meaning of the word and what it was used to actually express is lost. I certainly realize this is how languages evolve, but it is sad how the writings of a different age are never truly understood by those of later days.

What the movie also made me re-realize is how much times have changed. Now, everyone, like say an Allen Ginsberg, has an entourage. You can't get anywhere near them. I remember back in the day how you could just walk up to people like Ginsberg and speak with them. I did. We had a great conversation. I mean, there would be small gatherings in people's homes, coffee houses, or even places like *Griffith Park* in Hollywood. These gatherings would be formed around music or some cause, and people like Ginsberg, Pete Seeger, or *"Stephen"* Gaskin (God, probably nobody even remembers who he is or understands how important he was to the evolution of modern consciousness for the counter-culture generation), would be there and you could just go up to them, if you had something to say, and discuss the intricacies of life.

But, today it is all different. People are so full of themselves.

Not just the words of poets have changed. Life has changed...

___How Long Do Pillowcases Last?

I was doing a little spring cleaning yesterday, going through sheets and pillowcases, when I realized how long sheets and pillowcases actually last.

I came upon this one set of pillowcases. The backstory is, in 1988; I came up with this idea to tie-dye a set of sheets. Why, I don't really remember? But, I did it none-the-less. I actually very clearly remember doing it one afternoon. Anyway, the bottom sheet got trashed fairly quickly due to the encounters I had with various women back-in-the-day. I think the story of the final demise of that sheet is actually told in my novel, *L.A.: Tales from the Suburban Side of Hell.* The top sheet I used to wrap up my samurai swords as I took them to and from the set on the movies: *The Roller Blade Seven, Samurai Vampire Bikers from Hell,* and *Samurai Johnny Frankenstein.* I eventually tossed it after it had gotten torn and no longer washed clean. But, the pillowcases to that set, they were still in use, over twenty years later... I remember having them on my bed just a week or two ago. Though the tie-dye had faded, it could still be seen.

I smiled as I put them in the bag to give to the *Salvation Army.* Maybe they can provide some pillow coverings for somebody else for another twenty plus years.

Artistic Inclination

How many times when you speak with someone about the subject of the arts they say, *"Oh yeah, I used to play a guitar back in high school. I used to write poetry. I used to paint,"* etcetera, etcetera, etcetera... They key word term is, *"Used to..."*

When we are young many of us are drawn to the arts. We play music, we paint, we write, we do whatever... With age, the mundaneness of life takes hold, and we must do what we do to survive. For most, that is the end of any art. It is only a memory.

The key component of all of this is the fact that, *"The Arts,"* do not pay the bills. So, it is left behind. And, this is reality for most of us; no matter whether we still hang on to various elements of, *"The Art(s),"* or not; we must survive. If it doesn't pay the bills, then it often falls away.

This is very sad, I think. How the arts are a part of youth, but the world and society drives them away from us. If they do not equal money, time for them gets less and less.

There is also the other side of this issue. Many people get into the arts solely to become rich and famous. In our celebrity obsessed world; fame and fortune seem to be the pinnacle of human existence. But, believe me, as someone who has known many of the rich and famous, as well as many of those rich and famous who have fallen from grace; it is not the pinnacle of anything.

I have also seen the trend in many people who associate celebrity with life fulfillment. Again, it is not.

As a filmmaker I have often seen how people think that they are worthy of the highest honors of the craft, even if they have accomplished nothing. They assume Cameron, Spielberg, Tarantino, or Rodriguez will be knocking on their door tomorrow. As such, they feel they are too good to take the stepping-stone process of being in lower budget films to climb up the ladder. Of course, they never climb the ladder as no step was ever taken. Their egos held them back. So, they eventually stop being the waiter and going on auditions that they never to get and return to the Midwest (or wherever), get a job, and none of their dreams wherever lived. Just like all the others who had a glimmer of art in their youth, all they can say is, *"When I was young, I..."*

I have also witness people who wrote poetry and go very upset when the poetry magazine they submitted to expected them to subscribe to the magazine or pay a reading fee, if they hoped to be published. Now, poetry never paid anybody's rent. And, if they had shelled out a few dollars, at least they could have said, *"I was published..."*

This is the reality of art. This is the reality of modern life. Art takes energy. Art takes focus. Art may even cost you some money. But, if you follow your dreams of the arts, at the end of the day, it may equal something. Something as opposed to nothing.

Art need not be lost to the youthful. Art is art is art is art. It can survive youth. It can survive when it does not pay the bills. It can be what it is, art.

Art does not have to equal celebrity. Art does not have to equal fame. Art does not even have to equal money. Art can simply be what it is;

art. All you have to do is to keep doing it. From this, not only does the world become a better place, it also becomes a more artistic one, as well.

Live your art.

"I Coulda' Been a Contender."

"I coulda' been a contender," is one of the most memorable lines in the history of cinema. It was spoken by Marlon Brando in the film, *On the Waterfront.* This same sentiment is a feeling echoed by so many people as they pass through their life. There are things that they wish they had done but did not; things that they could've done but did not; things that they made one choice, but realized it was the wrong choice after the repercussions of the choice were long ago actualized. In many of these cases, what a person dreamed to accomplish was not actualized because of the choice(s) they made. They look back at their life and realize, *"I coulda' been a contender."*

The reality of life is this is an idea only expressed by those with a certain amount of age under their belts. The young have forever, so they never voice this thought. They believe there will always be a tomorrow, when whatever dream they hold can be lived. Even if you know this is not the case, and attempt to express it to them, your words are dismissed. Dismissed until, at a later stage in their life, they look back and realize that they did not achieve what they dreamed.

I have also heard the statement, *"I've wasted my god given talents,"* more than a few times. Similar to, *"I coulda' been a contender,"* this too is based upon a realization of choice. A person chose to go one way, chose to not work towards their dream, and they ended up where they never wanted to end up: empty and unfulfilled.

The entire, *"I coulda' been a contender,"* mentality is based upon the realization of choice.

We all make choices. The choices we make set the course of our life. In many cases, we never realize the absolute outcome of our choices until it is far too late to change the road we are walking upon. It is for this reason that the statement is made, *"You only get one shot."* Though in many ways this is true. It does not mean that you won't get a different shot. Though you may never be able to relive what you could have lived had you chosen the road to the left, that does not mean that a new set of choices will not be presented to you upon the road you choose to the right.

Some people also believe that choices were made for them. But, what people who believe this are overlooking, is that, as adults, we each choose our own path. Though you may not like the results or the outcomes of where you chose to put yourself, or where you ended up, it is you who initially chose to be in a certain situation or specific location. As such, you made the choice to set a group of occurrences into motion. Thus, there is no one to blame but yourself.

The important thing to keep in mind when and if you realize, *"I coulda' been a contender,"* that there is still life in front of you; there is still a chance to make your dreams happen. Now that you understand that you originally made the choice not to follow your dreams and the repercussions it presented left you unfulfilled, you must not make that choice of inaction again. You must choose to get into the ring and at least try to be a contender. Though you may get punched in the face a few times if you follow your path, you will have least gotten into the ring. From this you will know that you, at least, were a contender. Maybe not a champion, but a contender.

_____Look Before You Leap...

Yesterday afternoon I noticed a sign that announced the grand opening of a new Thai restaurant. So, when the evening rolled around, I went there for dinner.

It was a nice enough place with a patio overlooking the ocean, where they sat my lady companion and myself. I ordered up a large *Singha Beer*. My lady had a Thai iced coffee.

Before our food arrived, the Middle Eastern couple that they had sat us next to, had finished their meals. They were in their forties or so. As they waited for their bill, I sat in disbelief as they guy lighted up a cigarette and handed it to his date.

Are you kidding me? This is the twenty-first century! Smoking, especially around other people, is just wrong! Even if you are seated on an outdoor patio! And, it is, in fact, illegal to smoke in restaurants, at least here in California. I was really-really incensed.

I waited for the staff to say something. But, as they were all newly arrived Thais, and maybe because it was the first night of being opened, no one said anything.

As the woman glanced in my direction, I passed her a very hard stare. She glared back at me. But, come on, I was not the one doing anything wrong! How selfish and unthinking, I thought.

She eventually passed the cigarette back to the man after a few puffs. I proceeded to hard stare at him. I hoped he would hit me with the same glare that his woman did because, believe me, to a lady, even a smoking lady, I am a gentleman, but to a man, the gloves come off. I would have said something.

I could tell, he knew what I was thinking. And, though he didn't put out the cigarette, he kept it under the table and never made eye contact with me.

Their bill paid, they got up to leave. The lady stood up and came very close to the lady I was with. We initially thought she was probably just rudely studying the view, not taking anyone else into consideration. But, as it turns out, the woman was not studying the view. Instead, she had something very wrong with one of her legs and could barely move it, walk, or even stand on her own. In fact, it was so unmovable, her man-friend had to put his arm around her and guide her as she dragged the leg along one inch at a time as they maneuvered out of the restaurant. Any anger I had instantly turned to complete compassion. I felt very sorry for the woman.

This is the thing about life, had she not invade my space by rudely and illegally smoking, I would have felt nothing but absolute compassion for her. But, as she had done the unseemly, my first reaction to her was total distaste.

This is life, we are defined by what we do. We are defined by how we treat and behave around other people. In her case, she obviously didn't care what I or other people thought about her smoking. Maybe it was due to her physical condition? But, none-the-less, her initial actions defined how she was seen and perceived.

This is the case with all of us, our actions, our type of behavior, (good or bad), sets the stage for how we are viewed in life. What we do now, sets up our options for tomorrow.

As for the restaurant, the food was very good; obviously prepared by a chef. But, it was not Thai. It was more like some sort of California concoction. As someone who has spent a lot of time in Thailand and lived in Bangkok for a period when I was a radio station deejay, I can say that with some authority.

Nice enough place, but I probably won't go back. It probably won't last anyway. I have seen numerous restaurants come and go from that location.

Zen and Me

People often assume that I am a Buddhist. In fact, one of my publishers describes me as, *"A practicing Zen Buddhist."* Where they got that from, I'm not quite sure? I'm not a practicing anything.

Some people have also described me as a Hindu. I suppose that would be a bit closer to correct in that I was formally involved with Hinduism and was practicing and teaching the formal techniques of yoga and Hinduism in my youth. But, though I love Hindu symbology, it is not who I am.

I was born into a Christian family but that doesn't work either. And, let's not forget, I am an initiate of the Sufi Order, as well. For many years I was very closely linked to that group. But, that was in my younger days...

Perhaps one of my teachers, Swami Satchidananda, said it best, *"Truth is one, paths are many."* This same statement has been made many ways, by many people. But, it also misses the point—at least where I am concerned.

The fact of the matter is, I am really not into religion. Religion convolutes the truth and places all kinds of restrictions, expectations, definitions, and guilt upon people. I am against all of those things.

When I was very young, I walked into a bookstore on Western Avenue in Los Angeles. I was just looking around and I came upon a copy of the *Tao Te Ching*. For some unexplained reason, I was drawn to it. I opened it and read a few pages. It blew my young mind. I hurried home to borrow the money from my mother so I could purchase it. I still have that copy to this day.

If there were a written path that I believe is worth following, or at least drawing from, that would be it, the *Tao Te Ching*.

In terms of my interrelationship to Zen, I see Zen very much like the Tao. It is an abstract path to understanding and enlightenment. It is a path that only a few can follow, as it is so abstract. And, as the old joke goes, *"Abstract is my middle name."*

Those who follow the formalized path of Zen Buddhism, are not following, what I believe, to be True Zen. As formalized is never free. If it is not free, walking upon its path cannot lead you to enlightenment. So, I believe Zen is whole, pure, and true only onto itself.

The essence of Zen, *"Read between the lines."*

That's the story...

_____Process Verses Insanity

I went to pick up a latte' today. When I went into the establishment, I noticed that there was a lady adding milk and sugar to her drink. I ordered. As I waited for my latte' I observed that she was still adding, tasting, and then re-adding elements to her coffee. My latte' was created several minutes later. As I walked out the door, the lady was still there, defining and refining her drink; tasting it with each new addition.

As I have been speaking of late about, *"The Process,"* as a means towards enlightenment, I obviously took notice of her actions.

Now, it may seem like I talk a lot about things that occur at cafes. But, as I have long suggested, everyone should go to a café at least once a day and get whatever drink suits your preference, be it cappuccino, espresso, herbal tea, or whatever. For me, this goes back to my bohemian roots, long before *Starbucks* and the *Coffee Bean* even existed. But, any café is a place to take a break from the day. It is a place where things happen and people are. It is a place to observe and learn from life; i.e. this discussion.

My café sessions I talk about in little written pieces like this. My bar and juke joint experiences I leave for my poetry and novels...

Anyway... The aforementioned lady was really into making her drink just right. Making it a process, if you will. But, there is a fine line between process and insanity. This is perhaps one of the most subtlest elements of the spiritual path—knowing, which is which.

Perhaps the most ideal determination for this is why you are doing what you are doing. Are you doing something because you just can't stop? Are you doing it because you just can't get it right and you feel you really must? Or, are you doing it as a meditation?

As in all things on the spiritual path, there is no absolute right or wrong answer. Things just are what they are. Just as what you do is what you do.

This being said, think about what you do. Why are you doing it? And, does what you are doing lead your deeper into insanity or closer to nirvana?

Only Human

When George Stephanopoulos' book, *"All too Human,"* was released, I immediately understood what he was discussing. Though I never actually read it, (at least not yet), the book details his relationship prior to and after the election of President Bill Clinton, of whom I was a supporter.

All too human... This is the one of the essential components of life. We are all human. As such, we have all of the faults of being human. We have desires, egos, emotions, and all the etcetera.

The thing about the spiritual path, and particularly the eastern spiritual tradition is that it is taught that people can actually overcome these human traits; they can rise above them. In some cases, this is true. But, the reality is, as a human, all humans are human. And, you can only get so far away from who and what you are. No matter how hard you practice your techniques, you are still going to be defined by human traits.

The spiritual teacher or guru, particularly one who is no longer in their physical body, is always depicted as being completely pure and holy. They are always detailed as having completely left behind all forms of common humanness. The fact of the matter is, following the teachings of one of these gurus is very easy, because they are not around to see their flaws.

Some living gurus are also purported to be perfectly holy. But, if you hang out with them for any period of time, the flaws of their perfect holiness can be witnesses.

In some cases, the people who follow these teachers are so infatuated that they do not chose to see these flaws. Like young love, the person is perfect. But love, infatuation, admiration; all are emotions. So again, we go back to the root of humanity—we are all flawed with things like emotions.

I think one of the interesting things about the guru syndrome is how the followers of the living ones, (and in some cases the dead one), attempt to hide the flaws of these teachers. I remember there was this one western guy dressed up in the garb of a guru who used to have a school in Orange County. Maybe he still does? But, he apparently liked to watch baseball. He told his disciples he did this to help his food digest. When they told that to me, all I could was smile... I mean, how ridiculous. If you like something, do it! Don't make excuses about it! Even if you are a guru.

As a person who has walked the spiritual path for my entire life, I have always embraced humanness. I have embraced the flaws and, in some cases, relished in them; as can be seen in some of my novels. For me, that was always the perfect example of enhanced spirituality—being able to embrace the essence of humanness, while remaining conscious while engaged in any action; no matter how seemingly physical it may be. Though this is a hard path to walk, as most do not have the temperament, it is no different than traversing the spiritual path itself. For the spiritual path is abstract; ridden with potholes of illusion that appear to guide you but are only distractions on the pathway to enlightenment.

We are only human. If you want perfect holiness you will need to find it elsewhere.

The Process

In Zen there is always a lot of focus placed on the process. Whether this is meditation, meditative walking, making tea, or painting calligraphy, no act is ever just done. Instead, it is systematically prepared for and then precisely actualized. Practitioners of Zen feel that this is the best way to add to the overall experience, which ultimately leads them towards nirvana.

Most people simply jump through their life. They do what they do and that is that. Any planning is more based upon financial parameters than any level of consciousness.

Lord knows, I've written a lot about this subject—the subject of Consciously Doing as opposite to simply Doing. Though both can be a process of enlightenment, if you know how to live them, for many it is more beneficial to begin isolating a few areas of your life and start adding consciousness to their doing. From this, life becomes more refined, understood, and conscious.

These, *"Doing,"* things can be very simple and very ordinary. For example, if you drink coffee in the morning, instead of simply getting up and pouring it from the pot, take a little time to grind the beans, take a moment to pour the water into the coffee maker, then, if you have the time, watch the coffee brew. When there is enough for a cup, pour it into your chosen cup, sit down, and consciously enjoy this moment of enlightenment.

Though purists may say, *"Coffee? No way! Only the teas ceremony and the brewing of tea is the pure Zen path."* But, as anyone walking the path of consciousness knows and understands, consciousness is consciousness.

If something/anything, even brewing coffee, helps to focus and refine your consciousness, it is all good.

You see, Consciously Doing can be done anywhere, doing anything.

It is your life. How do you want to live it?

__Keep Your Feet Off of the Table!

I was sitting outside on the patio having an afternoon latte' at *Starbucks*, overlooking the ocean, when this teenage boy shows up. He was maybe thirteen. He grabbed a table, threw his backpack full of books on one of the chairs, sat down, and proceeded to put his feet not only up on the table, but pretty much extended his legs all of the way across it. A few of the other patrons took notice and gasped. Me, I smiled. It was amusing.

The boy sat there for a while. Then, his mother came up and told him. *"Get your feet off of the table!"* And, *"Let's go."* They had obviously set this as the place to meet when he had completed whatever post school activities he was involved in.

It is funny... If we remember back to our adolescences, there are moments when we each exhibited streaks of rebelliousness. We each put our own signature on doing something that we were not supposed to do—doing something against societal norms. It was our way of saying, *"Fuck you." "I am somebody." "I will do what I want."* I'm sure the boy's mother had her moments, as well.

But, it seems that in each of us, things turn around. Though we each keep our uniqueness, we decide that it is not right to put our feet on the table.

Good or bad, this is just the way it is. We leave behind the meaningless rebellion of youth and try to find solicitude in the accepted.

Though many claim they will never allow this to happen to them—that they will forever be rebellious, they will always be the rebel; this does not happen. Meaningless rebellious conflict just takes too much energy when you must spend your energy on navigating through the day-to-day struggles of life.

Nature

I spent the past few days up in Yosemite. On Saturday, I climbed to the top of Upper Vernal Falls. By the time I was on my way back down, it had begun to sprinkle. At the point I had return to the valley floor, it was raining.

No problem. I put on my rain jacket, and I was ready to go.

After I got my jacket, I looked to the road out of the valley, and there was, literally, a mile long (or more) line of cars leaving. I guess the rain sent them packing.

This struck me as very strange. First of all, the roads in and out of Yosemite are windy mountain roads. If you have a slowpoke driver, who is scared to drive this style of road, in front of you, it can really ruin the experience. But, more than that, there were a million cars leaving all at one time. No matter which of three roads out anyone of them chose to follow, it had to be a horrible driving experience.

More importantly, what is the reason that people go to Yosemite? Isn't it to be close to nature? Isn't the rain part of nature?

I mean, so what if you get a little wet. Doesn't it all add to the experience?

In any case, they all left. I stayed. I walked to a part of the valley I hadn't explored for a while. I found where a new makeshift river had formed.

As it has been a very wet winter in California this year, there is a lot of water flowing in Yosemite; filling the waterfalls, making cascades, and creating all of these really interesting small rivers. Me, I followed the river up and over the slippery, moss-covered rocks, and found its source. All this, as the rain continued to fall. This is nature.

How We See Ourselves

We each have a self-image. When we look in the mirror, when we think about ourselves, there is an image that comes to mind. But, is this image reality? Does the rest of the world see us in the same way as we see ourselves?

People judge other people based upon their own set of predetermined ideologies. They think other people should look and behave in the way that they deem appropriate. This is particularly the case, as one gets older. Elderly people get, *"Set in their ways,"* as the old definition explains.

I believe that this is a fairly obvious fact of life. Simply look at those people you know who are elderly and, in most cases, they have a pretty self-determined definition of how other people should look and behave.

If you watch people as they grow older, you can witness how most people tend to move away from any youthful style they may have possessed, into a more commonplace and commonly accepted style and behavior—which, undoubtedly, has been predetermined as appropriate by the society where they dwell.

People get older. People lose their style. They become the same as those around them. Any unique SELF definition is lost to the controlling hands of society.

This being stated, no matter where you find yourself in life, you dress in a certain manner, you wear your hair in a specific style, you talk and behave in the way you have decided you should. But, is how you see yourself, the way the rest of the world sees you?

Now, first of all, it is imperative to state, it doesn't really matter what anybody else thinks. If you are happy with yourself, then be yourself. But, is how you see yourself, the way you are perceived by others? This is one of the ultimate questions of life.

One way to judge this is, for example, if you see someone who is in your age range, and maybe they wear their hair the same as you, or maybe they dress in a similar fashion. How do you see them? How do you judge them? And, how does how you are judging them, reflect upon how the world sees and judges you?

Policemen wear uniforms. Firemen wear uniforms. Military personnel wear uniforms. Priests, nuns, swamis, all wear uniforms. Even businessmen wear uniforms: a suit and a tie. What is your uniform? And, why do you wear it?

How does it define you? And, does it depict, to the rest of the world, who you really are?

Loudmouth Loser

I believe that we each have encountered the loudmouth loser in our lives. This is a person who has accomplished nothing, yet they feel they have the right to spout off about whatever they feel like. When you present them with the fact that they have accomplished nothing, their answer always seems to be, *"Oh, but I will... I will..."* The fact of the matter is, however, they will not. Because people like this never do. They talk and talk about whatever they think or they believe; they may even attempt to force their opinion on you, but they will never do anything with their life.

In other cases, the loudmouth loser will state, *"I have the right to speak my mind."* With this, they may draw upon sources for this point of view. But, if they are quoting someone, they are quoting someone who has accomplished something. We know this because their words were recorded. Which means, their life actually meant something. This is not the case with the loudmouth loser.

I am always amused at how the Internet has provided the loudmouth loser with a forum. They can say anything and not have to answer for their words. They can speak to the world and hide behind screen names and millions of miles of distance, in a place in the ethereal realm where only an ip address exists.

Loudmouth losers always are the ones who, once they age, go after young people for their conquests of love and lust. This is because young people tend to be naïve, so they are more willing to believe anything an older person says—even if what they are saying is based upon lies and conjecture. This is one of the reasons I always say,

"Leave the young to the young. Let them live out their lives without the interference of the old."

I think we all have encountered loudmouth losers in our lives. Sometimes their nonsense may have even gotten to us and made us upset. But, the good news is, a loudmouth loser is all that they will ever be, because they do not have the wherewithal to actually go out and accomplish something. All they can do is spout their meaningless rhetoric hoping to upset someone to the degree that they will feel like they are something more than nothing.

The sage is silent.

Part of the Process

In life there is always a process. You rarely just get to go in and do it. Usually, you have to set up beforehand and clean up afterwards. And, this kind of sucks.

This also goes to the bigger level of things. You have to learn how to do what you're going to do before you do it, and this generally takes time. Sometimes a lot of it... Plus, you have to finish what you started if you want it (anything) to reach completion. This too takes time.

Then, sometimes what you did created such a mess that it takes a long-long time to clean it up and to get past it. If you ever can at all.

It's like painting. I love painting. But, it is very-very messy. Long ago I realized that I could never paint wearing any piece of clothing that I cared about. Because if you paint, you are going to get paint on your clothing, and there is no way to get it off once you get it on.

And, the clean-up. Awh man, what a mess... In fact, I didn't paint for quite a while, at one point in my life, just because I hated the clean-up.

Back in the day, when I was in my twenties, I used to live in this apartment in Hermosa Beach. It had a very big kitchen. What I would do is to staple gun a large canvas to the wall and paint it from there. I used oils a lot back then and the smell of oil paints and their toxic nature... Well, some believe it was what helped Van Gogh go insane... But me, I wouldn't clean up. I would just leave it. Sometimes the smell of oil paints permeated my apartment for days. I expected that it/they would sooner or later kill me. Well, not yet anyway...

Then there is music... The whole reason I quit playing music professional in live arenas is that I hated the tear down. I didn't want to end up being one of those guys at thirty-five or forty who had to cart their own amp on stage, set it up, and then carry it off once the show was done. At music shows I always think that kills the whole vibe, watching the lead guitarist pack up his own stuff and carrying it off stage at the end of a show.

Now, there is filmmaking. The lights, the gels, the setup, and the tear down. It all equals a lot of work. But, that's just the problem/the reality of life; we all have this stuff that we have to do if we want to do anything. For each person it is different, but it has to be done.

You can sit around and do nothing... As Zen as that may sound, it also equals nothing. So, if you're going to DO, you will need to set up and tear down. I guess we just each have to decide what we are willing to set up and what we are willing to tear down...

We each define our own life.

This is Reality

Reality is very simple. What you see is what you get. Though it is very simple, religions and superstitions attempt to feed all kinds of nonsense into it.

Religious and superstitions tell you all kinds of things about all kinds of altered states. They speak about this equals that. And, if you do this you get that. They detail that if this happens, it means that will occur.

Then, there are book written about religions and superstitions to make everything that is stated it them some kind of holy proclamation. From the writing of these books, those of later generations can quote them and claim that what they are speaking is the truth, based upon what holy knowledge has been written in the past.

Some people want to/need to believe all this nonsense. They are, in fact, programmed into believing it from the time of their birth. But, what is the difference between superstation and religion?

One person's superstition is another person's religion.

Think about how easy and free life would be if you just let all of this nonsense go and experience reality the way reality actually is; what you see is what you get...

Right Turn Only

I have this friend and she hates to make left turns when she is driving. She always asks, *"Can't we just make a right turn and go around the block?"*

Well yes, in some cases you can. You can make a right turn, go around the block, and then come to some intersection with a stoplight that will control the traffic and guide you on your way. But, in many cases, you cannot.

Have you ever thought about this? If you continually make a right turn, all you do is end up where you were. You go around and around the same block and get nowhere.

This is the life that many people live. They go around and around and around and around the same block. They do the same things over and over and over again. But, if you are afraid to make that left turn, you get nowhere; nothing ever changes.

Sure, sometimes it is a bit scary making that left turn—out across traffic to get to a place that you have never known. But, is it better to simply go around the same block, for all of your life, even if it is a bit safer?

No Outcome

You know, everybody has a design for their life. They have a vision of where they want to be and what they want to be doing. In most cases, it is somewhere else, doing something else than what they are currently doing.

This is the same with all projects that people undertake: whether it be drawing, painting, writing a poem, a novel, recording a song, making a movie, or repairing a hole in the wall. In their mind's eye they see it completed in some perfect state. But, in reality, it/life rarely ever reaches this level of perfection.

In Zen Tea Making, they spend hours attempting to make the whole process of making a cup of tea a meditation. The goal is to make the perfect cup of tea. But, is the tea made via that process any better than a cup that was produced in a couple of minutes?

I am so frequently bombarded by questions about what someone should do when something they are doing is not turning out the way they had planned. This may be their art, their movie, their book, their relationship, their trip to India, their whatever... They ask me, because people don't listen. I have said it time-and-time again, in so many ways, in so many places, *"If you have expectations, things will never turn out the way you planned."* This is the whole reason I developed Zen Filmmaking; because it allows the filmmaking process to become free—free from desires and free from expected outcomes. You get what you get and that is your movie. And, this is the same philosophy that should be applied to life if you wish to be happy.

Because I continue to get questions, let me say this again, *"No desire for a predetermined outcome equals freedom. Freedom equals contentment and happiness. Let go of your desired expectations and you will experience a much better life."*

Seeking

If you seek, you will forever be seeking; there will always be something that you do not know, something that you do not have.

This is particularly true with the spiritual path. This is how the greatest illusion of all time has been feed to the spiritual masses. For those who walk this path, there is always something out there: something unknown, something unhavable, ungraspable, forbidden—known only by the most holy.

But, who are the most holy? And, what makes them that way?

Again, another product feeding into the grandest illusion of all time—the illusion that someone else is more than you.

Most people seek spirituality at one point or another in their life. Some are drawn to it very young. For this, they are generally complimented. *"You are very pure..."* Others seek it when someone they love dies or leaves them. Most, wait until they are on their deathbed and then attempt to grasp onto whatever religious programming they were indoctrinated into—seeking guidance and assurance as they undertake the greatest journey of life; death.

No matter when it occurs, seeking is still seeking. It is looking for something that you do not have.

But, why don't you have it? Or, do you?

Have you ever watched a person die who is considered holy? They too have regrets. They too are left with the desire to complete unfinished projects, to do things, and the hope to live some more life. But, death cannot be stopped. They too die.

But, that's the point, when you are at the end of your road; you are at the end of your road. When you die, does your continued seeking prove anything? No, all it leaves you with is the unfulfilled desires to know more, understand more, and to do more. But, this is the same illusion that has been handed down throughout time: that there is something else/something more. But, the reality is, there is not. There is life and there is death.

People can feed you all kinds of further illusion that, somebody died for your sins, they are in heaven, they are watching over you, etcetera, etcetera, etcetera. But, the reality is, they have died. They are not here. You still are. So, no matter how much they are assumed to have known, it did not save them from the final life journey; death.

This is the problem with this death thing and how it feed into the ultimate illusion... People hope/desire to know what is on the other side. They, *"Seek,"* an answer. They want to know what to expect. They want a promise. But, all promises, all religions, all philosophies only feed you illusion. They only provide you with a reason to seek, not a reason to know.

The greatest illusion is that there is more to know. Those who want you to pay them for their supposed knowledge, propagate this. Those who want you to follow them, preach it. But, they know no more than you; they simply either believe that they do or they pretend that they do. But, the outcome is still the same. They live. They die. We all die. And, any promises made about an afterlife are only that; promises made. It is not here. It is not real. It is only a belief. A belief, is not reality, it is simply hope.

Think about this... How many religious, throughout time, have had completely different beliefs? Of course, your religion claims to be the, *"True religion."* But, don't they all? Think about it, if there was one absolute truth, wouldn't it be known and understood by all? But, there is not. So, stop buying into the illusion.

If you accept that you know as much as everybody else, right now you are free. You don't have to pretend. You don't have to pay anybody. You don't have to desire anything more/anything else. You don't have to seek knowledge.

Just relax into the fact that you know as much as they do, and you instantly become free.

_____You Will Forget This Moment

The reality is, you will more than likely forget this moment.

This is life. You live it. You experience its events. Then, most of them are forgotten. Only if a situation is a massive standout does it enter your long-term, recallable memory.

How many times have you been speaking to a friend, and they bring up an event that you totally forgot about? Once you are reminded; then you remember. But, had they not brought it up, you would never have thought about it again. For whatever reason, they remembered it and you did not.

How many times have you been speaking with a friend, and they bring up an old event? The only problem is, they remember it totally differently than you do. They put a completely different spin on it—different than you recall.

Again, this is life, and this is memory. People remember what was important to them—even if it wasn't important to you. And, people remember things in their own particular way, designed by their own unique set of life-parameters.

So, who was right? Did they remember the event the way it actually happened? Or, do you remember it correctly? This is one of the ultimate questions of life.

For better or for worse, I was blessed/cursed with an eidetic memory. Blessed, as literally I never read a textbook throughout college. I would simply remember my professor's lectures when I took the tests. Cursed, because way too much is located in the recallable part of my memory banks. There are way too many things that I just do not want to think about, but they are at the forefront of my mind.

Ever since I was a little kid, I realized I was remembering things that other people had forgotten. Ever since I had this realization, I began to fight this process. Whereas most people try to remember, I try to forget. And, this is the same for all of us. There are things we want to remember, rethink, and relive in our mind's eye. Then, there are all-kinds of events that we wish we could just forget. But, we do not. Some spiritual teachings promise a way to shut down the brain through meditation and the like. But, just like any life distraction: exercise, sex, going to the movies, whatever... They only work while you are doing them. Then, the thoughts, the memories, come back.

So, what are we left with? We are left with our memories based upon the life we live. What life are you living?

___Out of the Body into the What?

This little piece is predominately gears towards those of you walking the spiritual path, as the rest of you would probably have little interest in it...

In spiritual circles, there is always this discussion of, *"Out of the body experiences."* This, hand-in-hand with the fact that I have long discussed, *"Enlightenment is easy, but then what?"* brings me to a very essential point, *"What is enlightenment and/or why seek out of the body experiences?"*

You know, and, (for those of you who do know), I have written and spoken a lot on the subject of enlightenment. As I have a long said, *"People hold enlightenment off somewhere, in the unobtainable distance. This is the reason that they do not interact with it. When, in fact, it is the most easy and most natural place to dwell."*

Also, because people do not really understand enlightenment, they think that once a person realize their true, enlightened nature, then all life is going to be different, perfect, without a care, etcetera, etcetera, etcetera. But, think about this, once you merge with enlightenment, are you still not alive; which means, don't you have to eat, live somewhere, have bills to pay, and so on?

Most westerners are indoctrinated into the mindset of enlightenment by some eastern spiritual teacher or, at least, are presented with the vision that the guru, some guy with a shaved head or with long hair and beard, is the image of this state of mind. In the mind's eye, these gurus are always catered to by disciples, so all they have to do all day is sit around and meditate. But, believe me, if you have ever personally known a guru, this is hardly their lifestyle.

As mentioned, this is a subject I have discussed a lot and only a few people seem to get it. But, enlightenment is right here, right now, in the everyday. You can merge with it right now. Simply free your mind from the thought that you are not enlightened and instantly you find what the Japanese so aptly call, *"Satori,"* instantaneous enlightenment.

Now, enlightenment may not be what you think it is. But, this is the ultimate illusion of enlightenment. This is the supreme veil on obtaining enlightenment. As it has been programmed into your mind as something undefinable, unobtainable, or unachievable except by only the most holy, then you can never know it. But, there is only one reason for you not experiencing enlightenment, that is you expect it to be something that it is not.

Expectations is what holds you back from enlightenment.

We each have this supreme knowledge in us. Most people do not care about it and so they do not seek it out. Most of those who do seek it out, separate themselves from it. Why? It is simply their choice. They want to think it is far too distant to ever obtain. They want to hold onto the supreme illusion that enlightenment cannot be had.

I was watching this movie yesterday and they were speaking of out of the body experiences. They discussed the Tibetan Book of the Dead and how you separate from your body and look down on yourself, when you die. The funny thing is, this is exactly what I used to do as a young child. I could actually watch myself playing and doing things, like I was on a T.V. I would look down on myself, from above. This is also an experience that occurs sometimes when you take LSD. Now, I must say here, that I do not recommend LSD or any other hallucinogenic for anyone. When it is said, *"You are never the same after taking it,"* that is very true and this, *"Never the same,"* is not in a good way. So, don't do it! But, in any case, this is a common experience, while under the influence of a hallucinogenic—looking down and viewing yourself as if you were another person.

In spiritual terms, this is often referred to, *"The witness."* Where you are able to see yourself from afar. But, the reality is, this is all just Mind Stuff. Though it may be kind of interesting, it is not enlightenment. It is just Mind Stuff.

People who seek out and practice, this Mind Stuff are not walking a road to enlightenment, they are simply doing mind calisthenics.

You have to ask yourself, *"What does it prove?"* Yes, you can have an out of the body experience. Yes, you can travel through space and time. All interesting... But, is that enlightenment? No, that is just something to do in this Life Space.

Enlightenment is simple. It is easy. It just is. And, it is not hard to realize, self-realization. You simply have to turn off The You and merge with the one.

What's In It for Me?

"What's in it for me?" This is a line that I have used in several of my films. It was first used in *The Roller Blade Seven* as I kind of homage' to the nonsense that many of the actors were dishing out to Don Jackson and myself during the production. But, in reality, it has come to be how I feel about many things in life.

In interviews, I am often asked very similar questions. One of them is, *"What are your realization about your life?"* I commonly reply, *"Everybody wants something from me, but nobody ever gives me anything."*

When I say this, I am often asked, *"Why?"* Well, it is very simply. People always seem to want something from me, and they never want to repay the favor.

Now, first of all… I am always happy to help people out if I can. I guess it is based upon my early years of walking the spiritual path; being indoctrinated into selfless-service, karma yoga, and stuff. I guess it is also, just who I am.

That being said, I am constantly being stalked by people to help them out.

People always want something from me! They want to be in one of my films. They want me to finance their film or turn them onto people who will. They want to borrow my equipment. They want me to give them something I own. They want me to introduce them to somebody. They want to be in a relationship with me. They want me to teach them how to do something. They want me to distribute their movie or get them a distribution deal. They want me to help them with their book. Get them a publisher. Whatever... The list goes on and on.

One of the perfect examples of this, (that just came to mind), was this one guy. He was the audio-visual guy at a college where I was teaching a course on indie filmmaking. He also took the course. Seemed like a nice enough guy...

The weird thing was, after the course, every time I went into this one store, he would magically show up and tell me how much he wanted to be a part of one of my movies and how important it was for him to get his name on imdb.com, etc. I finally realized that he was having this one girl, who worked at the store, call him up whenever I would go in. That's how he would know when to show up.

At the point I was doing a local movie that I could use him in, I gave him a call. He showed up, did his job, and it was all-good. I got him on imdb.com. His dream was answered... Then, the next movie comes along. To save myself from being stalked again, I created a part for him and cast several people to support his character. I hit him up, let him know, but nothing... The problem was, due to his absence, I had to let the other cast members go as they had no one to play their roles off of. Finally, he got back to me after the production was done. *"Sorry, can't do it."* You see, he got what he wanted out of me. He was in a movie. He got his name on imdb.com. But, why bother paying back the favor?

This is just how it is with my life. I mean, now if a girl wants to show up and have meaningless sex with me for no good reason. Well, that's a different story. ☺ If somebody wants to give me a million dollars; all-good. ☺ If someone wants to hook me up with a new Rolex or a vintage D'Angelico; fine with me. ☺ But, that's the problem; everybody comes up to me and wants me to do something for them. Which, as stated, is fine, but sometimes I could use some help too.

And, this little ditty is not just about me. This is how most people are around the globe. They want what they want. They are willing to do whatever it takes to get it. But, once they do get it, they never say, *"Thanks,"* and they never repay the favor. They simply feel like they deserved it.

It's like, for example, everybody wants to get into the film business. At least here in L.A. But, the reality is, the film business is like thanksgiving dinner. Everybody is already seated at the table. There are no seats left. If you want to eat some turkey, somebody is going to have to get up and give you his or her seat. That means they are going to go hungry. Most people are not willing to go hungry. So, it virtually never happens. It is impossible to get into the film game.

But, it doesn't have to be this way. People can share. Please can say, *"Sit here with me. You take half of my chair and half of my turkey."*

From my personal perspective, I have always tried to help everybody that I could. If more of the world was like this, think how much better of a place this would be.

_The Stories You Will Never Know

There is a certain reality about life that most people never realize. That is, you will never know the true story. You will never know the whys. You will never know the hows. And, you will never know the reasons for.

Every element of life has its own unique story. Every news event has its own defining elements. Every person has their own unique tale to tell. But, you will never truly understand any of them.

Think about this. How many people truly know you? How many people know your deepest, darkest secrets?

When you describe yourself, do you ever share that part of you with anybody? Probably not. Most people only show very specific elements of themselves to other people that they know, let alone the people that they have never met.

When you describe yourself, you most probably put out an image that you want to be seen. This may be positive. It may be negative. But, in virtually all cases, it is not the absolute truth. It is they way you want to be seen by a specific person or the world as a whole.

This is true with relationships, as well. Inside every relationship, there are elements that only the couple understands. Other people may look and cast their judgments, but as they are not actually inside the relationship; living what they are living. As such, they never truly understand anything as they do not know the internal dynamics of that relationship.

This is just the same with all congregated elements of the world. Governments hide things.

Businesses hide things. Religious groups hide things. They all believe that a good portion of their interpersonal information is on a need-to-know basis. And nobody needs to know.

Even when the press investigates a person or a large conglomerate, they can only find out what they can find out. There are things they will never discover. And, there are things that once they are discovered, they do not publish because each news story has its own slant, defined by the journalist, the editor, and the news publication.

So, what does this mean for you? It means that you will never know the ultimate truth about anything. You can dig and dig, research and research, and you may find some answers. But, you will never know the whole truth, because there is too much hidden knowledge—concealed by each person who walks the face of this earth.

_____Make Things Better!

I am commonly asked the question, *"Hey Scott, what do you think I should do?"* My answer is always the same. And, it is always quite simple. *"Make things better."*

What does this mean? Well, just like the answer, it is very simple. Wherever you go, whatever you do—do what you can to make things better.

Now, I am not talking about some selfish act that makes your own life better. Nor am I saying do something based on some stupid religious ideology that your preacher told you was the way of god. What I am saying is that if you see something that needs fixing, fix it. If you see someone that needs help, help them.

For example, if you are in a store and one of the pieces of clothing has fallen on the floor, pick it up, put it back on its hanger, and put it back on the rack. If something has fallen off of a shelf, put it back in its place. If you are walking down the street and someone has dropped something, pick it up off of the ground for them. And, these are just a couple of examples.

Situations occur in each of our lives where we see things that we can do to make things better. Do them. It is as simple as that.

"Hey Scott, what do you think I should do?"

"I think you should make things better."

_____The Art Has Been Done

I was on my way to a music event the first year that the radio station Indie 103.1 was putting on their *Summer Concert Series* at the *Hammer Museum* here in L.A. Sadly, the radio station only lasted a couple of years, as they were very cutting edge. Though they are still on-line.

Anyway, prior to the show I was walking around the museum as they were having an exhibit about early abstract art. The first thing that I noticed is that the evolution of abstract art almost exactly followed my own development as an artist: the style, the technique, the subject matter, the freedom. What I came away with is how each of us, as an artist, evolves into our own unique mature styling's, but we all begin the same. This is especially true of, (for lack of a better term), abstract artists. We start by embracing a freedom of simplicity and then move forward into what we finally become.

As an artist, we are never a finished product. We each continue to change and embrace an ever-new and ever-evolving understanding of the images we wish to present. Though this is the case, as was so aptly demonstrated at this exhibit, we each began, as did the movement; embracing pure simplicity, and then we each move onto our own final placement.

_____Remembering When

I think one of the great and most interesting things about life is that we only remember when.

For example, you knew a person way back when and you haven't seen them since. This could be five, ten, twenty years, whatever. The image of who that person was is locked in your mind and they have never changed—they have never grown older. So, if you knew them when they were young, they are young forever.

In times gone past, before the age of the Internet, people really had very little means of finding a person and seeing what they look like in the now. Today, it seems everybody has a Myspace, a Facebook page, or a website. So, their NOW face is plastered across the ethereal plane. Something is lost with this, I think. Sometimes the memories are so much better.

Prior to the Internet it always surprised me when someone would come up to me years after I had known them and ask, *"Are you Scott Shaw?"* A couple times stand out in my memory. One was when I was in my first year at college. A guy I had known in junior high came up. He looked totally different, and we weren't even really friend in junior high. We just were in P.E. together. But, somehow he remembered me. Another time was in grad school. A girl I had gone to the sixth grade with came up. How she remembered me; my face, I do not know. But, she did… I would never have known it was her if she hadn't told me her name.

And, this is all good… But age, is a terrible master that controls us all. In many ways, it is so much nicer to remember a person back when.

_Everybody's Got the Same Hustle

You know, there is a sad reality about life. We all have to make money in order to survive. Life is a very material place. To survive you have to live somewhere, eat, and furnish your life with all of the additional items that you feel you deserve.

To reach that end, most people work the nine-to-five. Many hate what they are doing, but they do it none-the-less. Some people love what they are doing. And, that is great. That is the best way to live life.

But, there are those, and there's a lot of them, who are willing to do whatever it takes to get other people's hard earned money in order to finance their own lifestyle. Some may call it work. But, it is not. I call it a hustle.

Being involved in the film business, I have witnessed a lot of underhanded nonsense when it comes to money and getting money from other people. The stories I could tell you... But, in brief, people do a lot of really messed up things to get money from people. As there is the promise of fame and fortune in the film industry, people are easily sucked in by the promises. They hand over their money.

One of the main things I always emphasize about this issue in the classes I have taught and in my books and articles is that ninety-nine percent of the film industry is bullshit. People may want to make films, but they do not have the talent, the understanding, or the dedication to actually get them completed. But, they still hold casting session, from which actors and actress get their hopes up. The hustle money from investors, "If *you give me this amount, you will make millions. I promise!"* It is all a colossal waste of time and cash.

Then there is the other side of the issue, where people get money from actors and actress. The biggest offenders of this are acting teachers. I mean come on! If these people were actual actors, making money from the craft, then they would not be teaching. They are not working actors, so that is why they teach. But, people get sucked into it every day. They are told by the powers that be that they must take acting classes. And, a lot of money changes hands but the vast majority of actors never find themselves upon the silver screen.

Then there are the filmmaking hustlers. I have seen this so many times. For example, when I was first getting into the game, this guy who had made a few bad indie movies told me that his friend was the one who had made this super-famous actor, a star. How did he do it? He got him, (the actor), to finance a film in which he starred. Yeah right... He was obviously trying to get me to pay for his next movie. I passed.

But, I am not the only one this has happened to. It happens all the time. This is why I warn every novice actor, and particularly actress, who I come into contact with, *"Be very-very careful, who you hook up with."* Again, the stories I could tell you...

Perhaps the biggest problem with the film industry is that it is call an art form. It really is not. Like my friend Don Jackson used to say, *"The art is not in making the movie. The art is in finding the money to make a movie."*

Though, with the dawning of the digital revolution, it has gotten much cheaper to make a film, it still costs a lot of money. The bigger the movie, the more money it takes to make it. And, this is where the hustlers come out to play.

I guess this little piece is for the actors, actress, and filmmakers out there. If they ask you for money say, *"No."* No matter what the promise is, it will not happen. So, don't fall prey to the game.

Arrogance

The intricacies of human psychology always amuse me. As such, I often take notice of people as I watch life play out. I think people's behavior is very revealing.

I was driving down this side street on Saturday and this African-American lady walks out and into the street, mid-block. Now, this was not on the corner or anything... She proceeded to walk across the street about as slowly as I think it is possible to do so. She was wearing workout clothing, so you would think that she may have been coming from the gym, a power walk, or something. If she was, there was no sign of it.

The shortest distance between two points is a straight line; right? She, however, was walking about as diagonal to the two sides of the streets as possible. So, it took a long-long time.

Personally, if I am walking across a street and a car is coming, I speed up my pace to get across the street and out of their way. I think most people are like this. But, this woman didn't care. In fact, by the time she got to the other side of the street, two cars had backed up behind me. One honked. It served no purpose, however. She didn't even flinch or acknowledge the honk. If I could describe the look on her face, I would call it arrogant.

Arrogance... This is a funny emotion. And, it is always based in a misplaced since of accomplishment or the sense of deserving. *"I am this and you are not."* Whatever that, *"This,"* may be...

"I can do this because I can. Because I can get away with it."

"By doing this, it makes me something. Something more than you."

But, if you actually ARE something, you don't need to behave like this.

You see arrogance in a lot in people who have accomplished nothing but somehow, someway have decided that they are better or more than the people around them. Most people I have met, who have come from the bottom up, never exercise arrogance. Because they know what it is like to be on the bottom. The people who do practice this emotion, however, are usually the ones that were handed a life or a lifestyle and simply feel that they are deserving of it.

Deserving of what is the question: i.e. the lady who could take up everyone's life-time and walk as slowly as possible across the street, just to prove that she could. This is how arrogance is often played out.

In the neighbor where I live, I see a lot of arrogance. There is a lot of old money around here. So, the old people drive their old luxury cars, about as slowly as possible. They turn or stop when they want, wherever they want. They feel they have the right.

Of the younger crew, there are a lot of housewives who married a successful doctor, lawyer, or something, so they have nothing better to do with their time but shop and get in your way. I remember a few years back I was in the supermarket and about to grab some vegetables. This one lady, of the said variety, literally pushed her shopping cart right in front of me. I mean I was so close to the counter, my arm way extended, *"Hello!"* But, she was so rude and so arrogant that she completely dismissed that she had done anything wrong. And, told me so. I just shook my head and laughed.

This is probably the biggest point about arrogance, the people who practice it, are so locked into their own head that they do not even take other people's feelings into consideration, as they have decided that they are doing and can do nothing wrong.

And, in my neighborhood, the kids of these people... Oh my god, you can't believe what goes on with them and the way they behave.

You know, all of life is a choice. It doesn't matter how much money you have, how much fleeting beauty you possess, who you are married to, where you live, what you drive, who your parents are, where you went to school, who you know, or what guest list you are on. A conscious life is a conscious life. Living a good life, a respected life, is never based on negativity and/or exercising whatever small amount of power you may have over other people. It is about doing good things.

Good things are noticeable, just as bad things are. What do you do with your life? And, how do you behave?

Human Beings
Are Very Self-Centered Creatures

The reality of life is, human beings are very self-centered creatures. They only think about themselves. When they do think about others, they do it to equal their own desired ends.

Now, I do not mean to sound cynical here. Because, in fact, I am not. But, the truth be told, the only concern most people have is about themselves and those they have direct feelings for.

Why do they care about people they have feelings for? Because the see them as their possessions. And, they do not want their possession to become damaged.

Let's think about this for a moment... Remember the last time that the injury somebody incurred really moved you. Maybe you saw it on the news or read about it. You felt really sorry for the person. But, then a week, a month, a year passes—do you ever think about that person's injuries anymore? Probably not. If the memory does arise in your mind, it is only for a moment and it does not touch you the way it once did.

With the earthquake and tsunami that recently occurred in Japan fresh in our minds, attention has gone to the Japanese people. It is discussed how there is no looting taking place, as is commonly the case in western and middle eastern societies the moment something goes awry. There is no looting because they are a group-orientated people. This may be true. We are all indoctrinated by our cultures. But, the reality is, it has already been proven that the company responsible for the nuclear reactors has lied and has sent its workers into the plants, to attempt to control the leakage, without the proper equipment to even monitor the levels of radiation they are encountering. How, *"Group orientated,"* is that? And, who knows what other falsehood they have spewed? Only time will tell.

Why have they done this? Because they only care about themselves. They only care about the image of their company and the image of Japan on the world stage. And, I will not even go into the amount of lies that comes out of the mouths of government officials.

Religious leaders are no better. They do all kinds of things to stir up the pot and create disharmony directed against other religious or other sects within their own religion. They do this, in the name of God. I mean, God is on our side; right? Our side and nobody else's… I could go on-and-on about this, but the news does it for me. So, I will not.

On an interpersonal level, think about the people you have met in your life. How many of them were out for themselves? Out for themselves to get ahead, get what they wanted; and they do not care about the cost their actions have on others? I think a good percentage of the people, we have each met in our lives, have been like that.

Some people seem very good. They teach for small money, simply to help the children. They donate their time to animal shelters. The give blood to help the injured. Etcetera, etcetera, etcetera… But, why are they doing it?

Do you think that the teacher who earns far less wage than they deserve is not receiving some sort of reward for teaching? Does teaching not put them in a position of power over students? Are they not told by all their friends, what a good job they are doing—truly helping society. And, so on.

People who help the less fortunate in developing countries, ghettos, the reservation, get to feel that they are doing something for the greater good. That they are helping humanity.

And, this list can go on and on.

Even people who appear to be doing something good for no reason, have a reason. You may not know the reason. But, if you look below the surface, it can be seen.

For better or for worse, this is simply the reality of life, human beings are a very self-centered creature.

Why do you do what you do?

Be Willing
To Change Your Ideologies

I received an e-mail yesterday from a young filmmaker I communicate with. He had encountered some problems finishing up his latest film and asked for some thoughts or advice.

The only advice I can really give him, regarding filmmaking, and anybody else in regard to life, is that you must be willing to change your ideologies.

The reality is, in life, we each have a plan about how we are going to do something. In our mind's eye the situation occurs just the way we had planned, and the outcome is perfect. Even if we anticipate a certain number of problems, we feel they will be resolved, and it will all work out fine.

The reality of life is, however, there are a million sets of circumstances that we can never anticipate. These may involve people, mechanical items, nature, or even acts of god. Though we may have it all planned out, life happens, and it is rarely anything that we expect.

This is true of creative projects. It is true of interactions with people. And, it is true of living life.

If you stay locked into a predetermined pattern of thoughts and existence, the minute a new, different, or unexpected situation occurs, you will be lost and you will be upset that it did not turn out the way you hoped. Some people get mad at the people around them. Some people get mad at themselves. Some people get mad at life. Some people get mad at god. But, what good does any of that do? All you do is create a lot of, *"Upset,"* in your life. And, upset is not balanced, not happy, not creative, not free. It is simply stifling.

But, if you are simply willing to accept things as they come. If you are willing to change your mind. If you are willing to change your expectations, think how free your life becomes.

You Only Get One Shot

Have you ever noticed that when you fall asleep you start to dream about something. If you are awoken, in those first few moments of sleep, your dream obviously ends. Then, as you doze back off to sleep, you start to dream again. But, this time, your dream is based on a completely different subject. And, no matter how hard you may wish to reenter the previous dream, it is not going to happen. Life is like that; you only get one shot.

This is simply the reality of this place we call life. You have one moment to make a choice, live what you live, and set the next stage of your life into motion. If it is missed, (if you are awoken from your dream), then your entire life will evolve completely different. For better or for worse, this is the way it is.

Sometimes people and/or life situations cross our path. Destines intersect. With this, we either choose to take advantage of those occurrences and moved forward with them. Or, for whatever reason, we choose to move away in a different direction. In some of those instances, we regard that we did not make the choice to stay. But, that is simply the choice that we made. We had our one shot, and we blew it. There is no going back, no matter how hard we try.

The truth is, if you had lived that moment—made the choice to stay; maybe it would have turned out great or maybe it would have turned out very bad. Maybe, it would have turned into something you never expected. How many times have we each encountered those situations in our lives?

But, the reality is, you didn't make that choice. So, you can never live, what could have been lived.

Many people try to go back. They try to recapture what was/what could have been. But, that was then. This is now. And, a million life experiences took place in the interim.

In other situations, we actively pursue our dreams to reach a desired outcome. But, here again, once we begin to walk on a specific path, we encounter situations based in the randomness of life.

Plus, if we desire something; that, *"Something,"* is most probably involving other people. The moment you introduce, *"Others,"* into your equitation, all kinds of things occur. There are personalities, egos, individual desires, and interpersonal psychology. The moment other people come into a pursuit; the whole situation gets messy.

So, this is the complex pattern of life. Some would say that it is our karma or our destiny that hands us the set of choices that we are allowed to choose from. Maybe... Some believe that it is the mystical perfection of life. That we live, what we live, according to some divine plan. Maybe...

But, here is the reality... You only get one shot—one chance to make a choice from your set of choices. Do with it what you will.

Step Up to the Plate

As I was speaking about in my last blog, you only get one shot, so you really need to step up to the plate when a situation occurs and go after it.

If you haven't read that blog yet, you may want to read it first—it is the one just before this one. Or not...

Anyway... For some strange, unexplained reason, I was flashing back to a million years ago when I Swami Satchidananda's West Coast Soundman. Before every one of his lectures, I would show up with my sound system, cart it in to the arena, set it up, and test it out. Then I would load in my big and heavy, pro reel-to-reel and my cassette tape recorders. I mean it was the 70s, okay...

Funny, all of that equipment has gone by the wayside. But, I still have the microphone he used. He spoke many a lecture into it...

The one lecture I was remembering was in Santa Barbara. And, though he had his west coast ashram in Santa Barbara and his house in the nearby hills of Montecito, this was a highly attended talk.

Normally, I liked to be in the same room as him when he gave his lectures, to make sure the sound, sounded good. But, this night, in this hall, I had to station myself in a room off to the side of the stage and operate the sound system, change the tapes, etc., from that location.

The lecture and the sound went fairly well. I remember standing on my head for a good portion of the lecture. I mean, I was a yogi...

Anyway, after the lecture I was doing the tear down and this very interesting red headed yogi girl came up to me. She had a twinkle in her eyes. She said, *"I really appreciated all your energy."* What she was really saying, however, as it was quite obvious, was, *"I want to get to know you. I'm looking for love."*

At the time, I was kind of overwhelmed by the tear down, as it had to be done really fast, as there was going to be an after-lecture meeting at the ashram with Gurudev. Plus, I was brahmacharya. So, all I said was, *"Thanks."* And, I just let the moment pass.

I looked for her at other, future, lectures. But, I never saw her again.

This is the perfect point about what I was talking about in the previous blog. You get one shot; take it. If want something, go up and give it your best shot. If it works out, it works out. If it doesn't, it doesn't. But, at least you gave it a shot.

This girl did just that. She gave it her best shot.

The other side of the issue is going back, trying to recapture the, *"What could have been."* An ideal example of this happened to me a couple of years ago.

There was this very sweet girl from New York I had met in Golden Gate Park in San Francisco in the summer of 1976. We were all waiting for the Grateful Dead to show up and play. They never did.

After we met, we headed over to Yosemite and spent some time together there. Our paths crossed a few times in the latter part of the 70s and into the early 80s, but then we lost touch.

The great thing about the Internet is that people are findable. I get an email one day. It was from her. She was living up in San Francisco and she asked me to come up and visit her. Which I did.

But, you see, here is the problem—also as I discussed in the last blog... You can never go back to relive what you think should have been lived. In the case of this girl and I, we had our chance, our moment if you will; but that was a million years before.

In any case, the first time I went to hang out with her, she invited to meet her at this total hippie restaurant. You had to sit at tables with other people and stuff like that. You know, the whole communal thing...

She had something to eat. But, the fact of the matter was, the food looked so bad, and the place so dirty, I just had a cup of the Joe. I didn't want to get sick.

The situation was, she had stayed who she was back in '76; a hippie. Me, I was never a hippie. I was a yogi. But, I had moved on. Though all of my spirituality remained, I no longer had to wear it on the outside like a costume.

I hate hippies. I mean, grow up, get a life, take a bath. The 60s and the 70s were great, but they ain't ever coming back.

Now, I'm not referring to her, she was/is a sweetheart. I'm referring to hippies in general.

During our conversation, she even mentioned that she thought maybe I still was as I was—back then. But, I was not. For better or for worse, I had evolved.

Here again, is another point. This is something that I have long realized. When people are in a troubled relationship or they have not found an appropriate person to spend their Life-Time with, they look back. They look to people from the past. *"The one who got away,"* if you will.

And, this was the case with her. She was looking to the person I was, as her relationships had not panned out. She was looking to the, *"What could have been."* But, I wasn't that person any longer.

In fact, on my second visit to meet with her, she had taken some time off of work, as she wanted me to go to Yosemite with her; like we had down twenty-five years the pervious. Needless to say, I didn't go.

So again, to a point made in the last blog. You cannot go back. What is now is now. It is not then. Though new may be born between two people who met in the past. And, I certainly do not wish to negate that possibility. If you are looking for what was, it can never be again.

Both of these examples involve people, their desires, and their interrelationships. But, people are the starting point for where other desires are provided the opportunity to grow.

In regard to taking a shot... Both of the people mentioned did just that. They took a shot. And, that is the whole point of this blog and the previous one.

Taking a shot is your only shot at getting what you want.

Liar

Whenever I teach a course or a seminar on filmmaking, I always begin by explaining, *"What is the number one rule of filmmaking?" The number one rule of filmmaking is, "Everybody lies..."*

In the filmmaking industry, people generally lie to make their project appear to be more than what it is. Or, to make themselves more attractive to potential employers—to increase their value so they will get a new gig.

But, lying extends much further than the film industry. It is, in fact, rampant throughout all levels of society.

Why do people lie? The main reason people lie is, (just like in the film industry), they want to appear to be something more, something better, something bigger than what they actually are. They want to appear to be younger, older, better, more accomplished, whatever...

What is the root cause of this? The root cause is that people are dissatisfied with themselves. They are unfulfilled. They have not accomplished all that they hoped that they would in life, and they have not become that pinnacle of all that is right, great, and revered by the world. Lying instantly makes someone: something more, something else. But, it is not real.

The problem with lying, (and we have all done it at one time or another), is that you are left with the lie that you have told. All of the rest of your relationship with the person or persons you have lied to becomes defined by that lie. From this, you must struggle to keep that lie alive, which makes all of life complicated. And, a complicated life is just as mess. It is hard to live.

I mean, who wants to have to struggle even more through life, simply because you have lied? Life is complicated enough.

Many people committee what may be called a, *"White lie,"* a small lie. But, a lie is a lie, no matter the size. It doesn't make it right.

We have all been lied to. When we find out the truth, it doesn't feel good; does it? So, why do it to other people?

The fact of the matter is, there are a lot of people out there who live their entire lives based upon lies. They tell them all of the time and think nothing of it.

Most people who lie do so for selfish reasons. Guys want to hook up with girls. Girls want to hook up with guys. People want to be accepted into new groups. People want to climb the corporate ladder. And, as previously stated, people want to be more accomplished than they actually are; etc., etc., etc… It each case, a lie is defined by what is not—by who you are not. But, no matter how much you lie about it, no matter how much you may think the end justifies the means, it does not. Because if you lie, you are basing your entire existence upon falsehood. And, no truth, no true sense of accomplishment, no inner peace, no self-realization, can come from that.

If the reason you are lying is that you are not all that you want to be, do one of two things. The most spiritual of these is to simply accept who you are and embrace it. But, if that is not enough for you, continually move towards obtaining your end-goal. Stop making excuses and telling lies, and work hard.

The main thing is, don't lie to get there. Because, though a lie may open a door, it may also get it slammed in your face, once the lie has been uncovered.

A simple honest life is just bettered. It is easier, and more livable. Be who you are. Be what you are. Stop lying.

_____Don't Psychoanalyze Me!

I was sitting having an afternoon latte' on the outdoor patio at *Starbucks* the other day and I could not help but hear a conversation that was taking place behind me. There was this guy using all of this new-school psychological jargon. He was telling the woman he was with how she felt, why she felt that way, why she did what she did, and who she was. The suspiring thing was, after she contested his appraisals a few times, (from which he would immediately come back at her with more, *"Big Word,"* mumbo-jumbo), eventually she bought into what he was saying and agreed with him. How foolish she was? And, what a loser that guy was.

Have you ever noticed that whenever someone is telling you how you feel, why you feel that way, or why you act a certain way, all they are doing is describing themselves? I mean, I first realized this when I was in high school. It came to light when I was at a small gathering of friends on a Saturday night. We were sitting around this one girl's apartment in Hollywood and after we were done playing spin the bottle, we did that game where you tell people what you think about them. First of all, that is a real party killer! But anyway, my one friend begins to describe me. At first, I was thinking, *"You really don't get me at all."* But, then I realized, he was totally describing himself.

Similar things have happened to me a few times since. In most cases this type of critique is brought on when somebody is either angry or frustrated, as, I guess, it is their method to release their tension. But universally, whatever they have said, was wrong, and all they really did was describe their own psychological state of mind.

Perhaps one of the most curious or interesting times this happened when there was this middle-aged guy who took one of my filmmaking courses at *Santa Monica College.* After the course was over, he begged and begged me to let him be a part of one of my films. I gave in. Now, the reason I hesitated to let him on the bus, (as my filmmaking buddy Don Jackson and I used to say), was that I could tell he was one of those unaccomplished people who sabotaged every chance he had and every relationship he was in. I mean, he was alone and miserable, taking night classes in his fifties. Anyway, as could be expected, he got mad at me for some foolish nondescript reason. He called up my voicemail, psychoanalyzing me, telling me this and that about myself, and stating, *"You really don't like yourself,"* over and over and over. How wrong can anyone be. I love myself. ☺

Though he was totally wrong about me, what he did do was ideally describe himself. And, this is life. People want to project their own misery, ideologies, and psychology onto you. They want to think they know you. But, all they know is themselves. They do this style of projection as a means to attempt to control you.

Like that guy to that woman on the *Starbucks* patio. They do this to attempt to make themselves feel like they are something more. That they are a knower. They behave like this in an attempt to gain control; which, if they do get a rise out of the person, will make them feel like a whole and more. How sad is that?

A self-actualized, self-realized person does none of this. They let all people be who they are.

And, simply because they may have read a few books, took a few courses, or simply learned some key-words, they do not waste their time or energy attempting to tell other people who and what they are. Why? Because all they do is live in the perfection of their own Life-Time.

Ark Yuey Wong: To Fight or Not to Fight?

I find it very interesting that in my lifetime some of the very influential figures of the modern martial arts have come to be all but forgotten. An ideal example of this is Ark Yuey Wong.

Ark Yuey Wong is sometimes referred to as the Father of American Kung Fu. This is a well-deserved title. He had a studio in L.A.'s Chinatown on Ord Street and was one of the first Kung Fu practitioners to actually teach the art to westerners. Born in Canton, (Guangzhou), China, he spent most of his life in the U.S.

I first came into contact with him in the early 1970s. A couple of my friends were his students.

The early 1970s was a time when Kung Fu first became embraced in the U.S. Hong Kong Kung Fu films, such as *Master of the Flying Guillotine*, began to be seen in mainstream theaters, and the influence of Bruce Lee and the T.V. Series, *Kung Fu*, shaped the minds of the masses.

As has long been documented, most of my life has been influenced by the fighting arts and I first began formally studying when I was six years old. So, by the time I walked through the upstairs doors of Ark Yuey Wong's studio to watch my friends work out, I was about thirteen years old, and was no stranger to the martial arts.

Ark Yuey Wong taught the five-animal system of Kung Fu. He was a very nice man; in his seventies by the time I met him. Though I was not a formal student, he would often ask me to train in his classes and, in fact, personally ran me through many of the techniques of the animal forms that his school practiced.

Compared to the schools I trained in, his classes were very informal. Most of the students simply trained in their street clothes. But, some of his advanced Chinese students did wear the traditional Kung Fu training garb.

One night when I was at his studio, a new student entered the class; obviously drawn by all the Kung Fu kick-ass hype that was out there at the time. In fact, Ark Yuey Wong was feature as a practitioner in several episodes of the television show, *Kung Fu,* so he had more than a little something to do with developing all the hype. In any case, the man wore a white karate uniform with a yellow belt. So, he was obviously a novice student of the art that he had come from. About halfway through the class he asked one of the senior Chinese students to spar. Now, this is something that most people didn't or even today do not realize; there is no sparring in traditional Kung Fu. At least not the type that takes place in hard style martial art studios. In any case, the advanced student laughingly accepted. The karate guy got into his stiff karate stance and began to throw some baldly delivered kicks and some hard style punches. The student of Ark Yuey Wong's immediately went into a Kung Fu stance and shaped his hands into the praying mantis style. He poked at the new student a few times. But, nothing happened. There was no interaction. It was like watching two people doing two different dances at the same time. Ark Yuey Wong eventually ended the fight and told the new student to go and train.

The moral of this story is, what is out there in the media is not what is, in actuality, taking place in the schools that teach a specific art. What is in the movies is not what is actually practiced in the studios. But, that does not make it right or wrong. It just is what it is...

Could my friends who trained at the studio effectually defend themselves? No, not really. All of their effective fighting techniques were gain by watching me, where I trained in Hapkido and Taekwondo, or by interactive training with other hard style practitioners. But, that does not take away from what Ark Yuey Wong gave to the world. He was the first to train westerners in a soft style system of martial arts that was more about developing inner strength and a meditative mindset than simply learning how to kick ass. For this, he was a great man, is sadly missed, and should never be forgotten.

_We All Make a Deal with the Devil

First of all, I must preface this post by stating, *"I am not a Christian."* Though I was born into a Christian family and indoctrinated into the Christian tradition: Sunday School, etc.; like most religions, I find the history, evolution, and interpretation of Christianity to be completely lacking in purity or substance. This being stated, the mythical ideology of, *"Making a deal with the devil,"* or *"Selling your soul,"* seems very well suited to the way people live out their lives.

I think if we look back in our lives, we can all see a moment when we made a choice to live a certain way. And, that choice set a course of events in motion that has dominated the rest of our lives.

It is kind of like in the movies and in the novels, when the protagonist goes to the crossroads, where he or she meets the devil, and they tell him what they want. They are promised they will get what they desire, so they sign on the dotted line in blood. The problem always is, though they may get what they thought they wanted, the outcomes is never what they expected, and their life is not lived in the manner they had hoped for. Why is this? Because people can never anticipate the variables of life that eventually come into play with each life decision and/or choice.

When we are young, there is always tomorrow—there is always the chance to live our dreams. If it isn't happening today, it will occur tomorrow. So, we make our deals with the devil, to get what we want.

As we get older, however, we begin to understand that reality takes hold and we come to know that we may never get to be all that we desired, to live all that we had hoped to live, or to own all we had hoped to acquire. So, we are left living a life dominated by the choices that we made within our unique set of circumstances.

The point is, we make our life choices due to our individual life circumstances and what we desire. What we desire can be as small as falling in love with a certain person. It can be getting a specific job. Going to the moon, or whatever... Once we focus on that desire, what we then do is set about on a course to achieve that end goal. What happens in that pursuit is what defines our life. It defines our deal with the devil. We may say to ourselves, *"I really want that." "I really want to do that."* Or whatever... But, the choices we make, based in desire, is what sets a set of circumstances into to motion that defines the rest of our life.

Many say, *"You can choose to change."* Or, *"I have changed."* Not true. People are who they are. They may pretend to be something different that they may become for a moment or two of life, but they always revert to their own psychological makeup, defined by their unique set of desires.

We are who we are. It is as simple as that. So, where are you in your life? What deals with the devil did you make to get there? And, was the deal you made, worth the cost?

This is your life. Think about it.

_Don't Keep Your Horses in Cages!

In the neighborhood where I live a lot of people keep pet horses. I use the term, *"Pet,"* because they keep them locked up in small corrals and they are not allowed to roam free across the plains or, at least, in large pastures, as was intended. In fact, it is quite common to see people riding their horses down the trails that line some of the busy streets of this city. Sometimes, the horses are wearing blinders to keep them from becoming startled by the passing cars.

First of all, I feel sorry for all horses when they are ridden. Though there are all of these excuses that people make for doing so; the reality is, times have changed, and you do not need to ride a horse to travel from one place to another anymore. Horses are now solely owned for the whims and amusement of people. And that is just wrong!

More important is the fact that the horses in my neighborhood, (and I am sure in many other locations, as well), are kept in small stalls and only allowed to walk around a small corral for a short period of time each day. This is unnatural, unfair, and it is simply not right!

I have often thought to ask these horse owners if they would like to go through their entire life being caged like this. But, as I do not personally know any of them, I have not had the opportunity.

Today, as I drove past one of these corrals, two young girls were riding their horse's past on the adjoining trail. Another horse, which was in his cage, immediately moved towards the other horses.

I have often thought, as I have driven past this horse, *"He must be very lonely."* But, the girls riding their horse shooed him away. So much for his hoped for friendship.

People with money and people with their possession—especially when these possessions are other living things, really need to take a long hard look at themselves and what they are doing with their life and to the lives of other living creatures. Having fun or owning something simply to ride it, should never be at the expense of the life of another living creature.

The Only Bad Movies I'm In
Are My Own

As I have become fairly well known in the independent film game, both as an actor and a director, I frequently receive offers to appear in other people's films. Though I certainly appreciate all of the offers, I inevitably turn them down. As I always joking tell people, *"The only bad movies I'm in are my own."*

The reality is, people act in low budget, independent films based on two reasons. One, they hope to make money. Two, they need to be in a film to get tape on themselves to show their acting chops to agents and other filmmakers in order to move up the ladder. In my case, neither one applies.

The fact is, I am a member of SAG, the Screen Actors Guild. As such, I cannot be in a non-union film.

As virtually all films on the low budget, indie side of the picture are non-union, I can't be in one if I wish to maintain my relationship with and membership in SAG. I know many actors who have danced on the wrong side of this line, hoping to make some money, and they have all lost—they were kicked out of SAG.

As being a member of SAG is the only way to be in studio films, television shows, and commercials; membership is a must. They own the industry and you just do not mess with this powerhouse.

As an actor, periodically I have been luckily enough to appear in studio films, T.V. shows, and commercials. In terms of acting, that is my bread and butter. So, I want to say, *"Thanks,"* to all the people who ask me to be in their non-union indie films. But, *"The only bad movies I'm in are my own."*

The Scott Shaw Guide to International Travel
PART I

As I spend a lot of time out there on, *"The Hard Road,"* as I like to refer to it, I am often asked questions in regard to how to best travel internationally. To answer, here is, Part One…

One of the main things that I have to say, before I go into particulars is, look nice—dress nice. Westerners are commonly looked down upon, across the world, because they do not respect customs, and dress so shabby. This being said, what you wear at home, should not necessarily be your fashion choice for international travel. This is to say, if you dress shabby at home, because that is your style, don't do it internationally. So, forget about the tee-shirts, no matter how accepted they are where you live or how much they cost. Pack a polo shirt instead. They are just as comfortable, and they look so much nicer.

The reason for this is simple; there are a lot of restaurants, religious shrines, and even museums that will not let you in if you are not wearing a collared shirt. It is fine to be overdressed, but you should never be undressed.

This is the same with shorts. I never recommend wearing shorts. First of all, you will not be admitted into many places if you are wearing shorts. So, save yourself the embarrassment of being turned away. But, more importantly, they do not protect you from the sun, the elements, or even scrapes and scratches. When you are traveling you want to be able to experience all the sights and sounds as best as possible. So, you do not want to damage your body in any way, shape, or form. Wear pants!

This brings me to jeans. No!

Again, though you may wear them at home, you will not be let into many restaurants and higher end establishments if that is what you are wearing. No matter how much they cost. And, we all know, some jeans can be very expensive.

Why bother holding back your options, simply to embrace your style? There are a lot of very comfortable pants out there that are functional, while being fashionable, (if that is what you are after), while still being acceptable in all establishments.

Shoes... Since I was a teenager and throughout my adult years, tennis shoes have been my mainstay. I wear them with suits, tuxes, everything... Why? It is simple. They are comfortable.

Here in the States, culture and fashion is very different from many other countries. We, in many cases, allow room for the artist and the *fashionista*. Other cultures do not. They find it disrespectful if you show up in casual attire, like tennis shoes. For this reason, though I highly recommend you bring a comfortable pair for walking, have a backup.

Long ago, I realized if you want to wear tennis shoes to do all of your walking and you do not want to weight your luggage down with a traditional pair of hard shoes, there is a great alternative, dance shoes. Companies like *Capezio*, make black dance shoes that literally squish down to almost nothing in your suitcase. When you need to go out to a nice establishment, they look as good as any dress shoe.

The other style of shoes I recommend is, walking shoes. In the mid 1980s a company called *Rockport* and later *Dexter* began to make these shoes that were designed externally to look like dress shoes but internally they are like tennis shoes. In more recent years, companies like *Sketchers* have followed a similar path, but made the shoes much more fashion friendly. If you have limited space and want to travel light, go for a pair of shoes like these. Then, you can have comfortable feet while walking and still look good when you go out to dinner.

The main thing is, wear shoes that have a rubber style sole. You never want to wear shoes with a slick sole. And, for women, do not wear high heels. I can tell you from personal experiences, as I have been attacked a few times out there on the hard road, if you have to fight and kick someone in the groin, the head, or run, you do not want to be wearing shoes with slick soles or you may fall. You need to always be wearing sturdy shoes that you can maneuver in, and if necessary, kick ass.

This leads me to sandals and flip-flops. No! Do not wear them. They are not good for long walks. They do not look nice, and you will not be allowed to enter many establishments if you are wearing them. But, more importantly, they offer your feet no protection. If your feet are damaged, much of your trip may be ruined.

Also, always make sure your shoes are well broken-in before you bring them on a journey. A funny, (well not that funny), story happened to me in regard to this matter. Since they were introduced, I loved Nike hiking shoes. Every pair I had were very comfortable and durable. Just before I was on my way to East Asia, I purchased a new pair—assuming that they would be like all the other pairs I had. I arrived and began to walk. This pair destroyed my feet. As high-end tennis shoes were very expensive where I was, (in comparison to the States), and I couldn't even find a pair that was big enough, when I was finally willing to pay the price, my journey really suffered. So, break-in your shoes!

Since 9/11 the rules about what you can and cannot take on airplanes, in regard to shampoos, shaving creams, sunscreen lotions, and the like are continually changing. So, you will need to check that out with your particular airline before you travel. I can tell you about one experience I had. I was flying into Shanghai for an extended stay in the mid 1980s. When I unpacked, I discovered that my shaving cream had exploded. Now, this was not my first trip to Shanghai and I knew everywhere to go to buy necessary items. But, nobody had any shaving cream. What I ended up doing was that each day, in the shower, I would soap my face up and in association with the water and the steam I was able to get a pretty good shave. The point is, while traveling, you will forget things, lose things, or things will explode, and you will not have all of the amenities that you have at home. What you need to do is not shut down but explore your options and make new things work for you.

Many people either over pack or under pack when they are preparing for a journey. Both can cause you to not have an ideal travel experience. Here is my normal packing listing. I have used this for journeys that have lasted one week, to trips that have gone on for as long as two months. Though this clothing segment is designed mainly for men. (As obviously, I am a man). It can, however, be easily adapted for women. And, this list includes what I am wearing while I travel.

Here it is:
One suit (matching pants and a coat)
One sport coat
Two pairs of pants
Five shirts
Fire underpants
Five tee-shirts
Five pairs of socks
One pair of tennis shoes (running or cross training)
One pair of dress shoes
Two neckties
One belt, black
One pair of sweatpants
One pair of swim trunks

Here are the particulars of this list:
    Sport coats or suit coats are great for men (and women) because they allow you to look nice while carry necessary items in your pockets.
    Two pairs of pants (in addition to the one pair that is associated with the suit). You can intermingle them as necessary.
    Choose five shirts that you can intermingle and match with your pants and jackets. This way you will always be able to present a fresh look.
    One thing to keep in mind when choosing your clothing for travel is that dark colors and prints hide stains much better. As we all periodically spill things, and when you're traveling you may not have the opportunity to change right away, it is best to wear clothing that conceals stains. This is why solid whites and light colors are not ideal travel colors.

Five underpants. Wear either briefs or boxer-brief style. As you will probably be walking a lot, you really need the absorption of sweat provided by this style of underwear. Boxers just will not do it and you can easily develop a rash.

Five under or tee-shirts. Wearing an undershirt is something that I discovered in India many years ago. If you only wear a shirt, all of your sweat soaks through the shirt; then you and your shirt look very bad. If you wear an undershirt, however, all of the sweat is absorbed before it gets to your shirt. I personally wear tank tops. But, whatever style works best for you. It is your choice.

Five pairs of socks. Ideally, I recommend black workout socks, because they are absorbent, comfortable, and they look fine if you are wearing a suit. But whatever color or style you choose, it is best if they are all the same color. In this way, if you lose one, (as socks always seem to get lost), you can easily intermingle your remaining pairs.

The reason I bring one pair of sweatpants is that they serve two functions. One, you can sleep in them in association with a tee shirt. Two, you can work out in them with a polo shirt.

The swim trunks are obviously for swimming. They can also be used to work out in. And, if it is warm where you are, you can also sleep in them.

When packing all of your stuff there is an endless choice in suitcases. Choose what works best for you. One thing to not pack your items in, however, is a backpack. Across the world, everyone associates backpacks with hippies. And, nobody likes hippies.

A word of warning. Women do not carry a purse, particularly a designer handbag. There is a lot of thievery across the globe and if your purse is loose in your hand or on your arm, you are just inviting a purse-snatcher to steal it. If you must carry a purse, carry a small one with a long strap that you can wear over your shoulder and across your body.

There are also a lot of pickpockets out there. And, they are very good. You will never know that your wallet or your passport was stolen until it is too late. So for both men and women, if you are carrying things in your pocket, either keep them in deep front pockets or use the button to latch down your back pockets. This is the same with sport coats. Many sport coats have a button on at least one of the inner pockets. If you need to carry your wallet or passport with you, put it in that pocket and button it. Even if it is a bit of hassle to open and close it, it is worth the trouble to keep your items safe.

Okay, there you have it. The first installment of *the Scott Shaw Guide to International Travel.* Hope it helps and gives you some food for thought.

Buddha on the Net

Before the Internet was even called the Internet, and before scottshaw.com, I had two pages up in the early stages of what became known as the World Wide Web. One was, *The History of the Korean Martial Arts* and the second was a page providing links to spiritual pages which eventually became titled, *Buddha on the Net.*

The History of the Korean Martial Arts I put up because I was one of the first to truly study and document the modern evolution of the Korean martial arts. And, as I have long said, *"The original masters have continued to change their stories."* So, I hoped to place a frame of reference of the history and evolution of these modern schools of self-defense.

Buddha on the Net I created to provided people who were interested in studying or following the spiritual path a means to investigate the various sources of information and the schools that provided information on what became the web.

Approximately one year ago, I did a complete redesign of my website. What I had come to realize, in regard to *Buddha on the Net* and links to other sites, is that I had no control over their content. Some sites would change, and some began to propagate very negative ideologies. Some began to spew malware. Following in my own philosophy, *"You can only play in your own playground,"* I decided it was best to take down *Buddha on the Net,* as well as other pages on my site that provided links to other sites, as I had no control over what they had to say.

Recently, due to all the requests and questions of, *"What happened to Buddha on the Net,"* I have decided to put it back up on my site.

So, *Buddha on the Net* is back up, providing links to spiritual sites. I trust you find it helpful.

Comfort Women

I was joking with a friend last evening about the oncoming plume of radiation from the Fukushima nuclear power reactor and how it was scheduled to hit the shores of the western U.S. today. She said, *"Maybe they're finally getting back at us."* Referring to the fact that we dropped, *"The Bomb,"* on Japan to end World War II.

Now, I am a bleeding-heart liberal and I am against all forms of war, whether it is two guys slugging it out on the street corner or countries invading other countries. But, I could not help but think, when she made this statement, of all the negative karma Japan had developed in the modern era.

First of all, regarding bombing Japan. They started the war with us. We, the U.S., did not start the war with them.

It is like, I have this one friend and back in the day, as we were part of the first wave of Punk Rock, when we were in a club, he wound get drunk and go and pick a fight with the biggest guy he could find. Inevitably, he would get his ass kicked. I guess he still does this, as the son of one of his friends, who's thirteen, told me how he had to intercede when my friend instigated a situation at a car race and was getting his ass kicked. A thirteen-year-old had to intercede!

Now, this is the same as what Japan did in World War II. They picked on the biggest kid on the block. I am not saying what the U.S. did was right. In fact, I wasn't even alive yet. But, it did end the war, which ended the ongoing killing and maiming.

This brings me to the next point. Japan, from the early part of the twentieth century forward, was an expansionistic nation. They occupied Korea and parts of China, not to mention the Philippines, Indonesia, Guam, etc. In Korea, particularly during World War II, they forced women into sexual slavery for the soldiers. The translation for what these women were called is, *"Comfort women."*

Today, I was listening to NPR and they were interviewing the few remaining *"Comfort women,"* who are still alive. Instead of protesting the Japanese as was scheduled, they are sending their good wishes to them due to the quake, tsunami, and nuclear meltdown.

Do you know that Japan has never even apologized to these women? Yet, today, they sent their good wishes to the country. Who is the bigger person?

As anyone who knows me, knows; I have spent a lot of time in Japan. This may lead to the question, why? Well, first of all, I am certainly not one of those people who is all lost in the mythology of ancient Japan. Me, I fit in well with the crazy, modern culture of Japan, and particularly Tokyo. That is why I have spent so much time there.

I mean, there is all this heightened mythology that surrounds Japan. But, for example, the Samurai were gay pedophiles. Certainly, there is nothing wrong with being gay. But engaging in pedophilia, especially indoctrinated pedophilia, is a completely different issue. It is just wrong!

The fact is, many of the wandering Samurai traveled with a young boy to take care of all their needs, both physical and otherwise. Yet, this is a fact that years of propaganda has alleviated from the history books. And, that is just one example of the how cultural history is altered as time passes.

And, let's not forget the pilots who came be known as the Kamikaze. I mean, the terrorists who flew their planes into the World Trade Center and The Pentagon on 9/11 are still fresh in our minds. But, a half a century earlier, Japanese pilots carried out suicide missions by using their planes as bombs, killing themselves and an untold number of other people.

Plus, they still hold on to their horrible whaling industry and their slaughter of dolphins.

But, the point is, the Japanese have done a lot of damage that they have not owned up to. It was like, after getting bombed, they became the victim. But, they were not the victim. In fact, for a good portion of the twentieth century and prior to that, they were the victimizer. And, whether this is a person or a nation, sooner or later karma hits and karma hits hard. That is why it is so much better to try to only do good things. And if you do something bad, as we all do, at least try to make it right.

Rules of the Road

This afternoon I was cruising home from the LBC on the Vincent Thomas Bridge. As I was approaching the Pedro side, traffic came to a near standstill. This is very unusual on this bridge unless they are doing some sort of construction or painting it. As I got a little closer to the tie-up, I discovered what was causing the slowdown was a pretty young girl who had blown the front tire on her pickup truck, so she decided to come to a complete stop in the fast lane, get out, walk over to one side of the bridge, and call for help.

As I passed her, she had this face full of fear and was on her cell phone. There were truck drivers driving by giving her the, *"Hey baby,"* and honking, while others were flipping her off and yelling, *"Fuck you bitch."*

You know, blowing a front tire can be a bit scary. But, it is not a reason to simply park your car on a thoroughfare.

When I was sixteen, I remember blowing a front tire on the 101 between Hollywood and the valley. All I needed to do was to slow down, get off at the next off ramp, park the car in a safe stop, and change the tire.

The thing is, people do all kinds of things in life when they don't really know what they're doing—driving included. Sure, everybody passes a driving test and gets behind the wheel. But, very few people actually know the rules of the road and what to do when a situation occurs to them while driving. As they don't really know what to do, they meltdown, they freeze, they get scared, and they stop their car in the middle of a bridge; causing all kinds of problems.

You know, this is the same with all aspects of life. People do all kinds of things that they should not be doing, because they don't have the training or the understanding to do those things properly.

I'm a Nuclear Boy in the Nuclear World

"I'm a nuclear boy in the nuclear world," if I can borrow a line from a song by the band 20/20 which thrived in the L.A. club scene during the late 1970s and early 1980s. Sadly, they have become all but forgotten. If you can find one, check out their albums as they are (were) very good.

But, to the point...

Japan is erupting with a nuclear meltdown, due to the massive earthquake and tsunami. As someone who has spent a good portion of my adult life in Japan, it is very-very sad, and I feel for all of the people impacted by this catastrophe. And, it is only a few days old. The problems and the ramifications will continue to grow, at least for the foreseeable future.

If we step beyond all of the rational, that nuclear energy was the only logical course of action for Japan, (an energy poor country), we come to the fact, nuclear energy is bad. Have we forgotten *Chernobyl* or *Three Mile Island?* And, those are just two of the most prominent examples. People lives have been damage or lost by nuclear energy since the dawn of its creation.

Maybe most people do not remember all of the protests that took place against nuclear energy in the 1970s and into the 1980s. There was a reason!

From what took place at *Three Mile Island,* no new nuclear facilities have been built in the United States for the past thirty-nine years. Doesn't that tell you something?

From what has and is currently taking place in Japan, a few European countries have suspended operation of their nuclear power plants and are completely rethinking their usage. Again, what does that tell you?

What took place in Japan is still unfolding, as the earthquake struck only a few days ago. The first plume of radiation is scheduled to hit the west coast of the U.S. tomorrow. And, radiation is ramped in Japan. Plus, the nuclear reactors in Japan are still unstable and containment is nowhere in sight.

Just as with what happened in regard to the BP/Halliburton oil spill in the *Gulf of Mexico* last year, all promises were made that if anything happened it could and would be contained. People lie. Companies lie. Governments lie. And it is, we the people, that are left to deal with the consequences of a choice that we had nothing to do with making.

Change is Not Always for the Better

If you live long enough, you begin to witness how the world changes. And change isn't always good.

I was having breakfast at one of my main restaurant hangouts this morning, *The Kettle*, in Manhattan Beach. When I walked in, I realized that they had torn down the glass window shutters that housed the food server and coffee station, which is located on the patio—the only place I ever sit. As I consider several of the people who work there my friends, we discussed the situation. Universally, none were happy with the change. It exposed the coffee, the water, and the help to the prying hands of the passerby's.

Perhaps the most interesting part of this was that, maybe fifteen or sixteen years ago, I remember when they put the glass shutters up, just for this reason. This one busboy, who has worked there for the twenty-five years plus that I have been going there, was the only one to remember.

This is one of the problems with change; people forget the lessons learned in the past. As they are forgotten, they make the same mistakes twice.

Certainly, for better or for worse, change will happen. But, in change, even if it is considered for the better, something of the past is lost.

For example, when they build *The Grove* next to *The Original Farmer's Market* in L.A., they tore down all the very cool shops, antique and otherwise, that surround it. Though *Farmer's*

Market is pretty much the same inside, the moment you walk out, you are hit with a trendy monolith of meaningless materialism, where celebrities, the paparazzi, the wealthy, and the wanta-bes congregate. Lost is all the essence.

With time and change, businesses also go out of business. There was this great coffee house off of Hollywood Blvd., back in the day, called *Deja' Vu*. During high school, my friends from *The Sufi Order* and I used to hang out there into the wee hours of the morning, playing chess, talking, and learning from the wisdom of those of a different age and time.

In '82 a great French patisserie and cappuccino shop opened in Manhattan Beach, *Crème de la crème*. As I have always leaned towards the bohemian lifestyle, it was a great hang out, as there was no other place like it in L.A. But, by the early 1990s, with *Starbucks* taking over the world, it went by the wayside. So too was the case with this great patisserie at Roppongi crossing in Tokyo, called *Victoria*.

With time, things change. For better or for worse, in a few years everything will be different. But change, does not always mean that things are getting better—only different.

_____Filmmaking:
Keeping the Artist from Creating Art

As most of the people reading this blog know, I've made a lot of movies. Whether or not the people reading this blog have seen any of them, well that's a different story...

People often ask me, (because I've made so many films), *"How long does it take you to make a movie?"* The answer is, I have it down to a science. If I have a location, a cast, and a crew, I can shoot a movie in a couple of days, have it edited, and sound tracked in a week or so. So, within a month, the whole film can be in the can. And, in some cases, already released.

The reason I can do this is that I do everything. I do not delegate the jobs. I always have ideas, my equipment is ready to go, I am always working on new soundtracks, and I keep my software for editing functional and up to date.

The problem is, *the devil is in the details,* as the old saying goes. Ever since 9/11 it has become more and more difficult to find free locations to shoot at. Everybody thinks that you are up to something bad if you show up with a camera. And, you do get shut down. So, my lack of locations, in recent years, has truly hindering my filmmaking.

An ideal and somewhat amusing example of this happened to me when I went to shoot some stock footage in the L.A. Harbor. I didn't even have a cast or a crew. I was by myself. I was grabbing some shots and The National Guard drove up and before I knew it I was in those plastic handcuff things. I thought I was on my way *Gitmo*. They were telling me, *"We are at war..."* Luckily, they checked me out and figured out I was cool, no threat, and just a filmmaker. They let me go with just a stern warning.

The other problem is, as I have detailed in so many articles and books, here in L.A., everybody thinks that they are going to be a star tomorrow. And, this mindset has continued to get worse. So, there is a lot of misplaced ego floating around.

This is not just the case for actors and actresses, as you may expect, but for crew, as well. I cannot tell you how many times I have had an entire shoot day ruined by the cameraman. Yet, they remain all full of themselves.

Though I am personally a very meticulous cameraman, as I appear in many of my films, I need someone to shoot some of the scenes.

From this, the question is often asked, *"Why do I appear in many of my own films?"* Again, it goes back to egos.

With everybody thinking they are going to be a star tomorrow; you never know when somebody is going to get their panties in a bunch and walk off the set. With me in the film, I know I am going to show up and, therefore, can fix any problems with the story if some cast member leaves.

Outside of the industry, people don't realize all of these subtle particulars. This is how producers get people to invest in a film. Because somebody doesn't know what to expect, they expect nothing.

I know producers are always promising the investor everything: how much money they will make, how they are part of the greater good, how great the cast, crew, and director is. They are told they will get an executive producer credit and they pull out the checkbook. Everybody wants to be a part of the film industry, don't they? But, these words are all bullshit. Nobody makes big money on little films. Well, at least not the investors. Maybe the distributors...

The whole essence of my filmmaking style, Zen Filmmaking, is freedom and art. It is about removing as many obstacles as possible from the filmmaking process. But, the unfortunate reality is that times have changed. So, I do not make near as many movies as I could. Or, as some believe, I should. And, it's sad because all I need is place to shoot a film and a few competent and willing participants. I don't even need or want money.

By the way, I never take money from investors. It just makes everything too messy...

So, you see, every realm of art has it problems and its own set of unique circumstance that keeps the artist from creating. How long it takes for me to make a film is not the issue. The issue is, do I have a place and a posse?

_____They Can Say Anything...

I get a lot of e-mails. Very occasionally they are from people who have some nondescript, abstract, and misguided problem with me or with something I have said, done, or created. But mostly, they are very nice e-mails from very nice people. I am happy to read them. They tell me about a movie, CD, or a book that they or some other person has created. They invite me to an art or music shows. They ask me a question or invite me to come and speak somewhere. I like nice people... I think most people are nice.

Sometimes people give me the heads-up to things going on out there in the world that has something to do with me. In the e-mail that started this process, I was told about a review that was placed on Amazon.com about a book I wrote over twenty years ago, *Cambodian Refugees in Long Beach, California.*

Here is the review:

worthless, March 12, 2011
By sody

This review is from: Cambodian Refugees in Long Beach, California: The Definitive Study:
I have taught a course on Cambodian American refugees at various universities and found this book to be utter trash. The author comes to bogus conclusions concerning Cambodians in America based on almost zero research and questionable facts. Do not purchase this pathetic piece of sorry (borderline racist) op/ed posing as a *"study."* (If my review has

piqued your interest, skim through it at your local university library.)

As I had a few free minutes today, I thought that I would respond.

Hello Sody,

I just received an e-mail alerting me to your review on this book. First of all, I am curious, if you are a professor, why are you hiding behind a screen name? Why don't you use your real name, so we can know who you are and who is actually making these statements? I am also curious where have you taught courses on Cambodian refugees, as I know of very few colleges or universities that offer singular courses on the subject and I have been invited to speak at virtually all of them.

Normally, I do not become involved with reviews of my works. As we each have our own opinions—we like what we like and dislike what we dislike. In this case, however, I must say your review is very misleading and false. In fact, I am surprised that a professor, if that is actually what you are, would write such a review; as the research presented in this book has been extensively used and cited in many other studies, as this was the first book on the subject, originally published in 1989.

For you to claim the book is, *"Borderline racist,"* is false. Though you may not like the results that are presented within its pages, there is no racism involved. This book simply presents the information in a concise and unbiased manner.

For the record, my entire motivation for conducting this study was due to the fact that no formalized exploration, on Cambodian refugees, had been completed in Long Beach at the time I was involved with this analysis: 1986 to 1989. It was my hope that by presenting a factual and concise study, not only would it help the Cambodian community in their growth and assimilation but also shed light onto their situation in order for them to gain additional assistance and help to redefine the programs that were offered to refugees by the various aid organizations; as, at the time, they did not seem to be very effective. As such, this study was not based on racism. In fact, just the opposite.

You also claim that, *"Almost zero research,"* went into this book. This is also very un-professor like and blatantly untrue. In association with studying all of the available sources of reference, in addition to the U.S. census, city documents, and statistics—between 1986 and 1989 I spoke with every Cambodian refugee support group in Long Beach, in addition to every city agency that had anything to do with the Cambodian refugee situation. Then, in 1989, I went door-to-door and surveyed one thousand residence of the Long Beach refugee community. Though I interviewed one thousand people, I had to knock on over three thousand doors, as many people turned down my interview request and/or did not want to answer the questions on my questionnaire.

Also, though I initially wanted to present actual interviews in this study, the vast majority of the people I made contact with in my first session of interviews, in 1986, were against this. As such, I was forced to limit my questioning to a prescribed survey of approximately thirty-five questions. From which, I was able to create a quantitative set of statistical numbers which provides a concise understanding of the Cambodian refugee experience in Long Beach, California in 1989.

Sody, I did want to thank you for mentioning that the book may be found in university libraries, however. In fact, it is in many college, university, and public libraries. Not to mention it has been translated, at last count, into seventeen languages, and released around the globe. In fact, here in the U.S., I have seen a few different versions of this book. These facts therefore negate your claims of racism and that the book is an, *"Op/ed posing as a study."*

Finally, if you would, let us know who you are and where you teach. I think to possess that information would be very interesting.

_____Don't Talk to the Help

Whenever I go into the restaurants or stores that I frequent, everyone says, *"Hi."* They all know my name, and I know theirs.

There is this one lady who goes out with me sometimes and she asks, *"Why do you talk to these people?" "I never talk to the help." "Don't talk to the help!"*

She told me that one of her friends labeled her an elitist. That's a funny delineation but I think it pretty much suits her.

Me, I like to get to know people. Mostly, I think, it is because I am a curious person. I mean, everybody has an interesting life, a unique set of experiences, and a story to tell. From them, and their life-stories, there is really a lot you can learn. Plus, by nature, I guess I am simply a friendly person.

From my childhood forward, I have generally had good experiences with the people who work in restaurants and stores. Most of them have been more than nice. There are a few exceptions, however...

One of the first examples of the not so nice store experience, occurred when I was maybe fourteen or fifteen. I had walked over to the *Thrifty's* on Vermont—off of Hollywood Blvd. I needed some Testers glue to glue something together. I picked it up and went up to the front. There was an elderly lady working the cash register. When I put it down to pay for it she rudely asked, *"How old are you?"* I told her. *"We don't sell glue to people like you. You use it to get high."*

I mean, how ridiculous was that? Sure, by that point in my life, I had known people that sniffed glue. But, that is a complete brain cell killer. I would never do that!

Now, I know a lot of you of younger generations probably do not realize this, but if you had long hair in the sixties or the seventies, you were completely ostracized by the previous, mainstream, older generation. They thought we were all derelicts and drug users. How foolish.

Another occurrence happened maybe a year or two later. I had heard of this new music store over in North Hollywood on Laurel Canyon Blvd. I drove there as I was looking for a new Gibson SG. The SG was my favorite electric guitar through most of my younger years. And, I still really like them today.

Anyway, I go in the store and the guy had one, with a unique finish, hanging on the wall behind the counter. I asked to see it. He exclaims, *"The guitars aren't here for your entertainment."*

What a stupid guy. He was rude. He lost a sale. And, he soon went out of business.

A similar situation happened to me in the mid-1980s, up in Santa Cruz. By this point, I was financially established, no longer a teenager, and an avid collector of vintage guitars.

I went into a pawnshop as I saw a '66 Gibson Firebird hanging on the wall. I asked to see it. *"You got any money?"* The old guy behind the counter rudely asked. *"Yeah, I've got money." "Put $600.00 on the counter if you want to see the guitar."*

As I didn't have $600.00 in cash with me. I mean, how often do people carry that much money around with them? So, I pulled out several high-end credit cards. *"They charge us a fee for using those. I want to see cash!"* Said, the man.

The guy pissed me off. I walked out of the store.

As this was just at the beginning of the time when banks started to have ATMs, I drove over to the only one in the area—in the nearby town of Soquel. Unfortunately, it was Saturday afternoon, and as the bank was closed, the ATM didn't offer withdraws. My mind was racing about how to put $600.00 together on a late Saturday afternoon in a town I didn't live in, just to put that guy in his place. My girlfriend, at the time, told me to not worry about or be upset about the situation. Why should I give any money to that guy anyway? Why should I give him any business? I understood the logic in her words. I let it go. We cruised up to San Francisco.

The next time I was up in Santa Cruz, a few weeks later, I found a '65 Gibson Firebird, with a very rare finish, at a music store. Though it was $750.00, due to the fact it had a very rare finish, I was happy to pay the price. I bought it.

A year or so later, the pawnshop went out of business.

Perhaps the funniest of these experiences happen to me in '96. I was preparing to go back to K.L. (Kuala Lumpur) and Bangkok. I was on my way to pick up my tickets at Malaysia Airlines in El Segundo and I decided to stop at *Bullocks* because I needed a new wallet. The store was on Pacific Coast Highway in Manhattan Beach—the same street that Malaysia Airlines is on.

For those of you who may not remember, *Bullocks* was a high-end department store.

Inside, I found a wallet. Then, I decided to go upstairs, thinking I would look for a new shirt.

I needed to go upstairs because this store was laid out a little weird—the men's clothing was on the second floor.

So, with the wallet in my hand, I get on the escalator. As I begin to look at shirts, I notice that a security team has formed very close to me, complete with their radios on. I moved, they moved.

I mean, it was like a bad comedy movie, because they were so obvious. Everywhere I would go, they followed me.

There was a big burly white woman, leading the team. She was flanked by three or four male cohorts—all holding radios and dressed in street clothes, following my every move.

I can only assume they were thinking that I was going to steal the wallet. But, I was on my way to pick up First Class tickets to the other side of the world. So, believe me, stealing a $20.00 wallet was the farthest thing from my mind.

There was a part of me that was laughing hysterically inside, while this was taking place. But, there was another part of me that this treatment made very-very angry. I thought to confront the security guards and say, *"Are you following me!"* Then, put the wallet back and leave the store. But instead, I just let them waste their time and follow me around the store until I got bored with the whole process. At that point I went back downstairs, paid for the wallet, and left.

I told one of my friends the story about the *Bullocks Security Team* the next day. His statement was, *"You know, it's not the best or the brightest who work at that kind of job."* I guess that's true. But, in whatever you do, if you create negativity, between yourself and other people, all that is left is negativity. From this, nothing positive ever happens.

Sure, these employees may possess low self-esteem and are attempting to make themselves feel better by trying to exercise some form of nondescript power over other people. But, at the end of the day, they never grow from the experience. It has not made their life any better. And, it certainly has done nothing but created ill-will on the part of those they treated in this manner.

In fact, all of the people previous describes eventually lost their businesses and/or their jobs due to the closing of the companies.

The point to all this...

The people, the employees who exhibit this behavior, base their lives upon negativity and stereotypes.

I am sure each of us has a similar story where we were impacted with negativity unleashed upon us by some employee, somewhere.

What does this type of action equal? Well, first of all, it develops ill-will. And, that is never a good thing for a business. In fact, all of the stores, including the large chain-stores like *Thrifty's* and *Bullocks*, have gone out of business.

In each of our lives there is a time when we have authority over another person. What we do with that authority, is what sets the next group of events in our life into motion; be it positive or negative.

Negativity never breeds positivity. Negativity always breeds negativity.

Good is always good. Nice is always nice. It is as simple as that.

Do Something

Everybody has had the fantasy to be grandiose. To really succeed in life. To be a movie star, a rock star, a superstar athlete, a high priest, a whatever. Most people never move in that direction, however. They give up before they ever begin. Or, if they do begin, they enter the path with the completely wrong attitude. They expect to be at the end of the road, before they have even begun the walk. They want greatness, but they are not willing to go through the steps it takes to get there.

We've all heard of overnight sensations. But, the reality is, this is very-very rare. The rock star has practiced their instrument for years. The athlete practices and practices. The director has spent years mastering his craft. And so on...

But, the main point is, to get where you want to be, you have to do something. You cannot sit around and do nothing—expecting it to come to you. It just doesn't work that way.

Sometimes though, *"Doing,"* is difficult.

There is life and all of its nonsense taking hold of your thoughts, making you frustrated. There are relationships and all that they entail, distracting you. There is just a lot of life-stuff that keeps people from achieving.

One of the main stumbling points to achievement is people themselves. I have so often heard people say, *"I'm not good at that."* But, that's not true. You can be good at anything if you put your mind to. People choose to not be good at something. They do not try.

But sometimes, life gets a hold of you. Even me, I'm about as Type-A as you can get. Add some coffee to that mix and look out. But, sometimes I get so mad at myself. I feel so ineffectual. Things aren't just getting done as I had hoped.

What I do in those times is that I DO something. And, this is what I suggest that you need to develop—something that you can DO even when you are not feeling great about yourself or life. This can be painting, drawing, sewing, writing, taking photographs, poetry, blogging, vlogging, whatever.

It must be something that you do not have to strive to achieve, however. It should be something that is easy and/or natural, that you don't have to force. We all have those things. You just have to look for yours.

The main thing is, you must DO something. Because then, at the end of the day, you can look back and see and feel your accomplishment(s). From this, it will give inspiration to all other areas of your life.

And, you never know... You may become the greatest at what it is you choose to DO. And, from this, you may become grandiose.

Influences

For each of us, there have been people that have inspired us. What we do with this inspiration is our personal choice.

In some cases, we follow that inspiration and move towards our dreams. In other cases, we let that inspiration slip away; do nothing, and our dreams remained unlived.

Though there have a few people who have truly inspired me, there are a couple of examples of inspiration that stand out. In fact, they have come define my life.

The first occurred when I was about twenty-one years old. I had been, (for lack of a better term), an artist virtually all of my life. Though I painted and drew, something was missing. I could never actualize my vision. Then, I met a girl, who was also an artist. Though she was initially reluctant, as she was a very reserved person, she finally showed me her art. Bam! It hit me. Her art was so free and absent of formalized structure, that it just spoke to me. From that point forward, I have continually created art, refining my vision.

A second prominent example is when I met Donald G. Jackson. The how and the why of our initial meeting has been well-documented elsewhere, so I will leave that by the wayside. But, in any case, he asked me to star in a movie he was filming. On the first day of the shoot, he left the cast and the crew on the stage to fend for themselves, while he went outside to his car and spend an hour or two organizing his trunk. There was a part of me that said, *"Just leave! This guy is insane."* But, I never was one for rehearsal, so I just hung out and we talked while he played with all his stuff. Though that particular movie got shutdown, we eventually went on to make *The Roller Blade Seven* and a number of other films. During *The Roller Blade Seven*, I learn how to make an independent film with no money. Which, as soon as we completed the film, I went on to do *Samurai Vampire Bikers from Hell*.

The important point here is that though these people inspired me, it was I who moved forward and forged my own path.

Don often alluded to the fact that he really respected me. I believe the reason for this was that I took the ball and ran with it. Something that other people he had been involved with in the film industry, had not possessed the ability to do.

This too has been the case with me. Though I have showed the ropes to a few people, none have stepped up to the plate and hit the fastball. Some have spent the money and bought cameras and equipment, but they never finished what they started.

A funny story...

When I was teaching at this one university, I had a female student who actually turned out to be the cousin of a relatively successful independent filmmaker I knew. She went out and bought a very expensive camera during the course and really wanted to work with me. As I was about to do a movie, I invited her to shoot it for me. On the night before we were to go into production, I met with her to discuss any last-minute details. While we were talking, she takes out her camera and asks me, *"Can you show me how to focus it."* Obviously, I pushed back the production and found another cameraperson.

But, here's the point... We all have had people who have influenced and inspired us. It is our choice, not our destiny, what we do those influences.

This is your life. What have you done with your previous influences and what will you do with the ones that influence you in the future? Are you going to sit around and simply fantasies about living out your dreams. Or, are you going to take action and make them happen?

Your life. Your choice.

Hoarding

You know, with all of the television shows, currently in syndication, that chart the lives of hoarders and the damage hoarding brings to their lives and the lives of those around them, it is amazing that people don't get themselves together and stop it.

I guess, when you watch these shows, the hoarders are so lost in their own denial that they just don't get it. But, lives are being ruined.

I think most of us have known or at least have met a hoarder. Sometimes this comes in a sublet fashion. For example, I had this one friend that never invited me into his house. Whenever I would go to pick him up, he would be waiting outside. When he got near the end of his life, and wanted me to show him how to use the editing program on his Mac, I was invited in. This house was scary. Though everything was organized—boxes lined the house, floor to ceiling. Even in the hallways.

He didn't consider himself a hoarder, however. He considered himself a collector. He had thousands of CDs, DVDs, Video Tapes, Record Albums, and Comic Books. He thought they were all worth a lot of money. When he died, however, his wife had the comic books appraised and, even though many of them were quite old and quite rare, they were worth pretty much nothing.

This is the reality of life. Though you may place a high value on something and even believe it may be worth a lot of money; that does not mean that in actual reality, you can sell it for what you believe it is worth.

Another example is a friend of mine bought a very nice two-story house. He invited a girl from the apartment building he had been living in to be his roommate. Immediately, it could be observed that she was doing, what most would consider, very obsessive collecting. For example, I was told that she would buy a book. Then, she would photocopy the book and keep the book and the photocopy.

There may have been some logic in that process to her, but to everybody else it would appear very unnecessary.

Once, I made the statement to her, *"Why don't you get rid of all this shit?"* I am told she got very angry with me. But, that is what hoarders do; they justify their own misguided actions.

Eventually, this friend stopped inviting me into his house. When I would pick him up, he too would be waiting outside. I knew why...

Today, when you drive by the house, sometimes you can see boxes and boxes and boxes pouring out through the window blinds. Like my other friend, organized, but simply an unlivable mess.

The problem is with hoarders, as can be seen in all of the television shows, not only are the hoarders psychologically glitched in some manner. But, their actions not only ruin their own life and their own future but the life and the future of those who are around them.

For example, I can only imagine what the life is actually like for my friend who owns this nice house but has been unable to bring people into it for years. I am sure it destroyed his chances of having a serious relationship with any other person. Thus, he hasn't been allowed to married or have a serious long-term relationship. I truly feel for him because I know his life could have been better and he deserved it.

Now, this is not a judgment thing, because I understand the process. Earlier in my own life, I was quite a collector. By the time I was in my early thirties I had five cars, a Harley Davidson, literally hundreds of guitars that I kept in a temperature-controlled storage unit, dozens of Swiss watches that I kept in a safe-deposit box, and thousands of books.

Hoarders always seem to have a motiving factor that sets them to collecting. Though I didn't think about it at the time, mine was probably due to the fact that there was a lot of loss in my childhood. I mean, my family moved a lot. I went to either eight or ten grammar schools; depending on if you want to count the ones I went back to. I went to four junior high schools. So, I too had my misplaced logic for collecting. I was trying to grasp and hold onto something—anything to give me a sense of permanence. Luckily, I caught myself and I cleaned house.

Today, I'm just the opposite. I embrace only items that provide an absolute necessity. And, I feel so much better. So much freer.

The fact of the matter is, all hoarders, (or collectors), have their logic for doing what they do. But, the minute what they are doing is negatively affecting the lives of others; they really need to step back and do something about it.

In fact, hoarding is one of the main factors that drives people into extensive debt. They keep buying to feed their need—whatever that need is. They do this, while, in the process, destroying their own life and the lives of all those around them.

The simple fact of life is—no one can do anything for you. And, you can't do anything for anybody else. You can talk, yell, scream, criticize, analyze, and make somebody feel guilty, but until they are ready to make a change, no change will ever be made.

I remember watching one of the first documentaries made about a hoarder living in San Francisco a few years ago. Again, the stuff in this lady's apartment was acutely organized. But, it was an insane mess. The landlord and the city had stepped in at one point, put a dumpster below her window, and through everything out. Then, she recollected an entirely new collection. Finally, they evicted her. But, she preferred being homeless than parting with her stuff.

The reality of hoarding is, most hoarder have people who enable them or they make enough money to enable themselves. But, that does not make it right. The minute someone else is negatively affect by a person's hoarding, the entire game changes—because then the hoarder is unleashing all kinds of negative karma. They are affecting the lives of others in a negative way.
And, that is just wrong.

A funny story to conclude... A number of years after I got rid of my massive library of books, I received an email. This guy contacted me, as he was a collector of rare books from India and he had just purchased a large quality from some other collector. They all had, *"From the Library of Scott Shaw,"* stamped in them. He wanted to know had they been mine, as he felt if I had owned them and/or brought them back from India, it would somehow add value to them. Well, the value part I questioned. But yes, I had owned them. And yes, I had brought them back from India on various journeys.

So, as you see, the process goes on. But, you do not have to take part in it. You do not have to be a part of it. This is what living a conscious life is all about. You must take long, hard looks at yourself and define the rightness of your own life and your own actions. You must try to make this place we call LIFE a better place and do all you can to help people and make their lives better, not worse.

Free yourself. Stop Collecting.

Oblivious

You know, most people are oblivious to the affect they are having on other people. And, in most cases, they just do not care.

Think about how many times you have been driving down the street and the person in front of you is talking on their cell phone, texting, talking to their friend sitting next to them, yelling at their kid in the back seat, putting on makeup, eating lunch, or whatever, and they either cut you off or are complete blocking the flow of traffic. Do they care? Probably not.

And, the old people who are way too old to be driving and go zero miles an hours in front of you. Oh my god... They're too old to care or to even understand that what they are doing is just wrong.

Or, the old ladies at the supermarket who don't even take their checkbook out of their purse until their order is completely rung up and then take forever to write their check. It's the twenty-first century people. Nobody writes checks anymore!

I mean, people's oblivion goes to all aspects of life. For example, a year or so ago I was walking into a store and a lady outside, in her mini van, starts honking her horn right next to me. She was honking at her son inside the store. She wanted him to come out. It was one of those really loud horns. It actually hurt my ears. It startled me and I said, *"God damn it..."* as I was sticking my finger in my ear to block the sound. Then, she rolls down her window and proceeds to tell me that I am rude for speaking like that. Are you kidding me!!!

Today, I was having breakfast at *Farmer's Market* over on Third and Fairfax. I guess it is now more properly called, *The Original Farmer's Market, as* there are so many places selling street groceries that are referred to by the same name. But, this place is both a market and a place to have some great food. It has been around since the 1930s and I have been going there all of my life. In the mid 1980s is when I guess I became a regular. Anyway, you can find me there, eating at the Belgium waffle place, in the AM, a few days a week or having a *coffee-hottle* from the coffee stand over by *Bob's* in the early afternoons.

Anyway, back in the day, there was this elderly lady named, June, who used to run the waffle shop. Somehow, she decided that I always wanted the waffle with strawberries and whipped crème on it. How she came up with this realization, I never knew. For, in actuality, I preferred another one of the waffles they had. But, she would see me walking up and my order was in.

Maybe ten years ago, the shop was sold to a crew originating from the Philippines and they added crepes, sandwiches, and other stuff to the menu. Me, I guess June knew something I did not. I have stuck with the waffle with fresh strawberries.

But now, you have to put your own whipped crème on if you desire it. The whipped crème container sits on the counter.

With all the weird diseases that flow around this planet, I can be a bit paranoid about people touching what I am eating. I remember back, maybe ten years ago, when I was going out with this lady and her younger brother tagged along. We went to a restaurant and he ordered a burger and fries. When he finished pouring the ketchup onto his fries, he licked the top of the bottle.

I never used ketchup in a restaurant again.

Anyway, today while I was waiting for my waffle these two East Indian ladies got their order before me. They actually grabbed the whipped crème and took it to their table. Though this really is not the way things are supposed to happen, the workers let it go. As I sat there reading the *L.A. Weekly*, I looked up and witnessed the one lady licking the remaining whipped crème off of the top of the whipped crème spout. She then carried it back and put it on the counter. Again, are you kidding me!!!

Now, a teenage boy you can be more forgiving of, performing this style of action. But a fifty something adult....

Anyway, I asked for some fresh whipped crème when my waffle came up.

But, let's face facts, the majority of people of this world are oblivious to what they are doing and how, what they do, affects others. All they care about is themselves and fulfilling their own momentary desires. Are you like that?

Personally, I truly attempt to take other people and other people's feelings into consideration while I am doing anything. But, look around, this is rarely the case.

How do you behave?

Selling Your Religion

For fun, I sometimes go to thrift stores. I see it as kind of my distraction in life. Because you never know what interesting pieces of cultural memorabilia you may find in these locations...

Anyway, today I stopped at one over on the sketchy side of the tracks. Sometimes these are the most interesting.

When I was walking from my car, I noticed this white guy who looked a bit out of places as this was in a part of L.A. that is predominately Latino. Out of place also, because he was dressed different than the surrounding people(s), wearing slacks, a dress shirt, and tie.

Well, I guess if I'm using that standard, so was I. As I was wearing my traditional garb: slacks, a long-sleeved shirt, (untucked, of course), a sport coat, and tennis shoes. Anyway...

When I came out of the store, I see him across the parking lot sticking flyers under the windshield wipers of cars. When I got to my car, I see there was one of his flyers under my windshield wiper. I looked. I smiled. He was selling his religion.

It was a rather high-end flyer, with info about a Baptist Church. I thought this was kind of strange being a predominately Latino area. As Latinos are almost universally Catholic. But, it did get me to thinking. I mean, what was he attempting to do? He was attempting to draw people into his church. And, why do people try to draw people into their church? One, they think they have a better religion, and/or a better way of presenting a religion to people. And two, they want their money.

I mean, never lose sight of the fact that churches charge an attendance fee. They may call this a donation. But, without those donations, the church would cease to exist. So, are churches not non-profit as they claim? No they are a for-profit entity.

Now, I know, I know... A lot of people out there feel they are receiving wisdom from their preacher by attending his sermons. Some even feel they are receiving inspiration and guidance from god. But, think about this; remove the middleman from the equitation, speak to god directly, and then, not only will you be in direct contact with your own source of inspiration and guidance, but you will also not have to take part in the process of selling your religion.

____It's All About the Benjamins, Baby!

Whenever people think about actors, they commonly assume that they get paid a lot of money. This is, no doubt, due to all the press on those actors at the top of the A-list who get paid millions and millions of dollars per picture. Though I commonly tell people this is rarely the case, few believe me.

It is the same with writing. People believe that simply by getting a book published, the author instantly becomes a millionaire. Again, as I commonly tell people, this is not the case. Unless you are Stephen King, Anne Rice, or J.K. Rawlings, the fact of the matter is, you don't make a lot of money from writing a book.

Below is a great example, regarding acting... Here is a statement and residual check from two 1991 Warner Brothers films I was in: *Bonfire of the Vanities* and *The Player.*

Bonfires of the Vanities was either the second or third film I audited for when I decided to become a actor rather late in my life. I was thirty-two. I got the part. It was a small scene with Bruce Willis. The scene ended up on the cutting room floor, however. And, since the movie was such a critical disappointment, I doubt that they will ever release a special edition of the movie with deleted scenes. But, I did get my SAG card for being in that union film.

The director of *The Player,* Robert Altman, personally asked me to do a cameo in the film. (Well, actually his people contacted me). This was a big honor, not only because it was a Robert

Altman film, but also because it was an over-all great movie.

I got paid what is known in the industry as, "*Scale*," for appearing in both films; which worked out to be about $550.00 per day at the time. I was on the set of *Bonfire of the Vanities* for three days. *The Player* was a single day shoot.

But, to the point... Look closely; the residual check is made out for a whole, whopping, $0.79. That's seventy-nine cents. And, I get to look forward to those checks rolling in once a year.

It's all about the Benjamins, baby! It is all about the Benjamins...

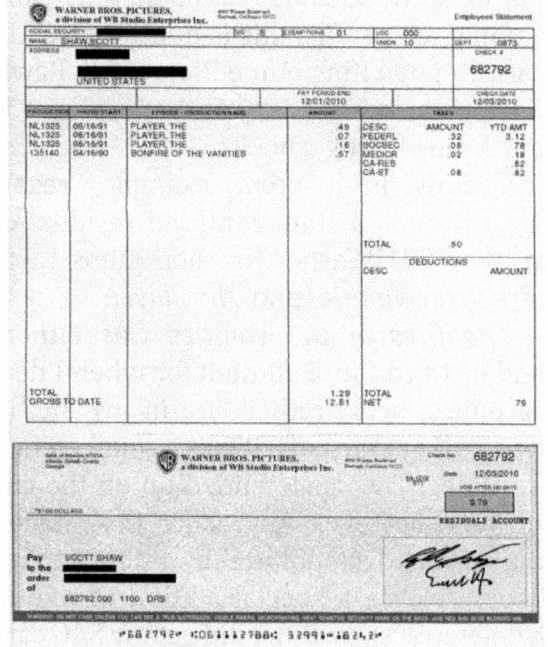

Trapped By Circumstance

In 1983, when I was in graduate school, they had re-released the movie, *Last Tango in Paris*. As I had never seen the movie upon its original release, (I was too young as it was rated X), I decided to go and see it as it had become a modern classic. It was playing at only a few theaters around L.A. One of them was on Wilshire Blvd. in Beverly Hills.

I had a few hours to kill this one early afternoon before my classes were to begin in the evening. I remember I invited my girlfriend, but she was mad at me about something. I had probably done something she didn't like. In any case, I went by myself.

I saw the movie and was on my way out when the man who took my ticket at the door, asked, *"Are you Scott?"*

As it turns out, he was a guy I went to high school with. In fact, in high school, we were friends. We often walked to school together.

In high school, he was one of those really smart people. I mean, you could just sense his intelligence. I really felt the guy was going to go far.

Me, on the other hand, I was anything but a good student. My mind was far more fixated upon my work with *the Sufi Order, the Integral Yoga Institute,* playing music, traveling up and down the coast, and following a few other abstract roads to spirituality that most people did not understand.

When we were in high school, he lived in a bungalow apartment with his parents a few blocks from where I lived. His father was a longhaired projectionist at a movie theater in Hollywood. That seemed like a pretty cool job back then. Plus, he had long hair, which was more than unusual among parents of that era. It meant that he, *"Understood,"* and that he was cool.

But, more than that, his father owned one of the first synthesizers in the home that I had ever seen. He was pursuing a career as an electronic musician.

I had long been enthralled with electronic music since its birth. His father was a true inspiration to me. Wow, I thought, you could actually have your own synthesizer in the 1970s. As soon as I could afford it, I bought one. My first synthesize was a Roland SH 3. I wish I still had it.

In the lobby of the theater that day, after we got reacquainted for a moment or two, he asked me what I was doing in life. I told him I had spent some time in India, was in graduate school, was teaching the martial arts, was writing, pursing music, and so on. I had no intention of creating this affect, but I could see his face drop. He, in fact, made the common, *"You're doing all that and I just work here at a theater."* I guess it didn't help, but I explained to him I thought that he would go on to college after high school and do something big. *"There's still time, man!"* I exclaimed. I mean, we were only twenty-four years old.

For those of you who may not know, here in California, in the 1970s, up to the early 1980, the community colleges were virtually free to attend if you were a California resident and had a high school diploma. All you had to do was buy your books. Anybody could and should go. I did.

I mean look at me, the bad student, who was far more focused on other aspects of living life. I went through the community college system, transferred to a university, and had ended up in graduate school. But, my one time friend never choose that path. He had followed in his father's footsteps.

Now, this may be a bit hard to understand for you who grew up in other places. But, in Hollywood, there were the haves and the have nots. There were those who lived in the Hollywood Hills, some of them in virtual palatial mansions. And then, there were those of us who lived south of Hollywood Blvd. Like my friend and I. We were the ones born of the working class. Not the children of producers, directors, industry moguls, rock stars, deejays, and movie stars.

"The Haves," whether they were smart, talented, or not, seemed to be presented with a path paved in gold. The others of us... Well, we were not.

Except in one case... A situation that truly motived me in life.

Back when I was in school, junior high was three years: seventh through ninth grade and high school was three years: tenth through twelfth grade. So, our first year at Hollywood High was tenth grade. I know it has changed since then...

The first year, there was this guy, who lived up in the hills, who scored with a couple of the prettiest freak girls on campus. We referred to ourselves as, *"Freaks,"* back then because we had long hair and were more or less ostracized from society. You know, we were the drugies and the etc...

This guy dropped out in the beginning of eleventh grade. One day, early in the twelfth grade, I see the guy. His long locks are gone, and he is wearing a green jumpsuit. He had become a janitor at our school.

Now, certainly there is nothing wrong with being a janitor. It is a needed profession. But, not only did this guy come from money, his future could have been joyous, if he had only played the game. He didn't. Thus, the guy who had it all in tenth grade, by the twelfth grade, his road to the stars was over.

Now, believe me, being who I was and involved in the numerous off campus activities that I was, I had many times pondered dropping out of high school. Seeing this guy, however, sealed the deal. I would finish high school and do something with my life.

But back to the main subject... After we spoke for a few minutes, I left the theatre. I never saw my one-time friend again. At least not yet...

I really felt for the guy, however, because he was a good dude that could have truly succeeded in life. But, he was trapped by circumstance. I'm sure he needed to get a job after high school to help pay the bills. There was probably no time for college or pursing whatever dreams he had.

In my life, I taught yoga and the martial arts. So, I could make money while remaining more or less free to pursue my life goals. Sadly, it is not this way for everybody. They are trapped by circumstance.

I believe that we need to think about this whenever we question why someone has ended up where they have ended up.

_____You Never Know
Who You Never Knew
That You Knew

I think it is always funny when you find out who (or more properly whom) you knew that you never knew that you knew...

As many of you know, I was born and spent my adolescent years on the wrong side of the tracks in Hollywood, California. One Saturday, I was sitting around at my friend Venchinzo's, Venice Beach apartment, pounding down some brews, as we tended to do. He, like I, grew up in Hollywood.

Our exploits are well documented in stories in several of my novels and poems.

In any case, we were watching T.V. this day, waiting for the night to come around when we would go out to a bar or a club. He was flipping channels and a movie featuring, Leonardo DiCaprio came on. We watched it for a few minutes and he said, *"That's Leonardo."* I answered, *"Yeah, I know, Leonardo DiCaprio." No. That's Leonardo." "What!"* I exclaimed. *"That's Leonardo!"*

When we were teenagers, Venchinzo's and his family lived in a court style apartment building on Garfield Place in Hollywood. A couple of doors over from his building was another court style apartment building. This is where his cousins lived. In this court, there was a little boy named Leonardo. He often played with one of Venchinzo's distant relatives, a little girl named Gypsy. And, we all occasionally with these kids.

When Leonardo was rising to fame, I never knew he was the same little boy we used to play with. In fact, I knew his mother, Irmelin and his father George, who used to deliver adult newspapers. But, I never realized…

Another similar story is, there was a girl I went to high school with named, Lisa. She was a grade behind her sister Debbie and I, but we were all friends.

Again, I was kicking it at Venchinzo's one day, drinking beer, and a Prince video came on MTV. *"Didn't you go to high school with her,"* he asked. (As Venchinzo is a couple of years younger than I). *"Who?" "Her… Lisa Coleman." "That's Lisa!"*

I didn't even realize it, though I had, of course, seen Prince's videos, even watched the movie *Purple Rain.* (By the way, she was the longtime keyboard player for Prince). But, I never realized that was the same girl I went to high school with.

In fact, before I had a car, her (very cool) mother used to drive us around in her Volkswagen Thing, (for those of you old enough to remember that model), with personalized license plates that referenced the primary chemical ingredient in marijuana. And, after I got my license, I used to give her rides sometimes…

After living in the valley during college and returning to India for a second time, I moved to Manhattan Beach, while I was in grad school. There, I used to rent videos from a place called, Video Archives. Though I never thought much about it, I used to rent videos from this one very hyper, skinny guy, who talked a lot. Later, after he became famous with his movie *Reservoir Dogs*, and discussed his early life and where he worked in interviews, I realized I used to rent videos from Quentin Tarantino.

Though I doubt that he remembers me, just like I didn't remember him... I'm sure to Tarantino, I was just another guy in the South Bay with long blonde hair. But, it is just an interesting set of circumstance.

Maybe even more interesting is the fact that the production offices we used for the first full-length feature film I produced, *The Roller Blade Seven,* were the same offices, used by Tarantino, when he was doing *Reservoir Dogs.* He had moved out. We moved in.

Every now and then someone comes up to me and says, *"Hey, aren't you Scott Shaw. I took a seminar from you way back when... Or, I studied martial arts at your school in..."* Sometimes I remember them, sometimes I do not. But, I guess that is the great thing about life, you never know who you never knew that you knew.

The Learning Annex

The Leaning Annex is a company that organizes education programs and puts together classes for adults that promise to help them in their career and overall evolution through life. In the early 2000s, I taught a few classes for them. There was always a problem...

Initially, the first class I taught for them all seemed to be working out very well. It was a class on independent filmmaking, of course. They provided me with a large auditorium in Santa Monica. Over one hundred people attended the class. In fact, it went so well, I didn't even have time to show the class examples of some of my Zen film work and the works of others, as I normally do at the end of a class. This was due to the fact that there was so much class interest, discussion, and participation.

One of the interesting experiences of this class was that one of the participates, a young girl from Texas, who had come to L.A. to get into films, blurted out. *"I want to be in one of your films. I'll take my top off!"* Everyone chuckled, including me.

Though the girl and I got together and had drinks to disuse upcoming projects. And man, that girl could drink! Just the way I like 'em. She drank round-for-round with me. In fact, she insisted on a few more rounds. But, nothing ever came to pass with her being in one of my films, as she seemed to following a career more along the path of becoming a film extra rather than an actual actress. I through that was unfortunate, because she had a great look and presence—something that is essential for an actress.

In any case, *the Leaning Annex* promises to pay their instructors within thirty days. The preverbal check was never in the mail, however. So, I called them. They explained that the company had recently changed hands and I would be paid someday. That someday never came. Though they, of course, took in all the money from the one hundred plus participants that took my class.

A few months later, they asked me to teach another class for them. I'm a forgiving sort by nature, so I looked at the first class as simply karma yoga. I agreed.

The next class, they did not provide me with the promised T.V. and VCR, however. And, the class was located at some horrible hotel in Marina Del Rey. Plus, they gave the class no P.R. So, there were maybe fifteen or twenty people in it.

The class itself went fine. I believe the people learned something. But, I was thinking, *"No more..."*

Again, thirty days passed, and I wasn't paid. I called and they made all kinds of excuses and were pretty rude to me. But finally, a month or so later, they did actually send me a very small check. Not the amount that was promised. Whatever...

In 2002 I was teaching at *Santa Monica City College. The Learning Annex* in San Francisco had heard about me and called to see if I would teach a class for them. I told them about my previous experiences with the payment situation, but they promised it would be different up there. Reluctantly, I agreed.

The class was well publicized, and it was held in a banquet room at a four-star, central city hotel. I made reservations to stay at the same hotel, drove up there, and was all set. For dinner the night of the class, I walked across the street to this 50s style diner, and all was good.

Class time came round, and the students began pouring in. *The Learning Annex* even sent a very pretty Asian girl to check people into the class and/or to have them pay the appropriate fee if the participants had not prepaid. All good. The only thing they forget was that I needed a chalkboard to write on. But, they fixed that problem by getting me a very large manila paper tablet set upon an easel.

I kept all my scribbles on those pages for a time, thinking I would make it an artwork. But eventually, I tossed it.

The class was over-full but it went great. The next morning, I made the five or six-hour drive back to L.A., as I had a class to teach in Santa Monica that evening.

The problem... Time passed. No payment. I called. Again, verging on the rude, they made all kinds of excuses. They told me they lost all the paperwork. *"What!"* I exclaimed, *"You even had a girl signing people in." "Yeah, but we don't remember who she was." "What!"*

Eventually, post a number of phone calls they decided to pay me the minimal amount for teaching a class. This, when it is their policy to pay their instructors per the number of students that attend a class. Thus, I got screwed by them again. My plan was to never teach for *the Learning Annex* again.

The funny thing is, a few years went by and they called me to teach a series of three classes for them in San Francisco. *"No thanks."* I told them the story of how they had ripped me off every time I taught for them. But, I don't think that they heard me.

A month or so later, I was bouncing around San Francisco. My lady and I were going to have lunch at *Johnny Rockets* on Chestnut Street and I saw a stack of *the Leaning Annex's* booklets in a paper machine on the street. I grabbed a copy and looked through it as we ate. There it was, a photo of me and a description of the class I was to teach. *"Are you kidding?"*

Anyway, I was obviously a no-show for that class. They called me up all angry, *"Why didn't you show up? The class was full."* I let them talk to the voice mail.

They were angry with me when they had screwed me over, not once, but three times. I mean, come on...

But, what is even more ridiculous, with me not showing up for the first class, is that they started calling me the next month, for the second class that they had me scheduled to teach. They were telling my voice mail how it was sold out, how they couldn't wait for me to teach, etc., etc., etc.

I didn't show up. Of course, I got the angry phone calls again.

But, then comes the third month, for the third class, and the same thing takes place all over again. I mean, how ridiculous is that!

You see, this is the absurdity of life and the nonsensicalness of the powers-that-be. They want to control you. They want you to serve them. When you get smart, and you don't serve their needs any longer, they get mad at you.

The sad thing is, most people find themselves dominated by these powers-that-be throughout their life.

Most people want to be something, they want to achieve something, they want to do something, but they cannot, because they are controlled by these external forces that, in actuality, have no idea what they are doing. And, in fact, these powers don't care. They don't care what affect they are having on you. All they care about is that they have a job, that they are doing what they want to do, and that they are getting paid.

Though I know it is a difficult life situation, my only thoughts on this subject are to try to step out of this pattern and devise a life where you are the only one having control over you.

The Leaning Annex... I guess, for me, it fulfilled its purpose. I learned to never work/teach for people who don't possess the honor to stand up to their promised commitments.

No Rehearsals

I was in El Segundo a couple of days ago. My lady was enthralled with this bead store. So, I decided to go and take a walk around the old section of the city, as it had been a minute since I had been there. Just as I walked past this open front restaurant, I see a guy and he says to people sitting at all the tables, *"Okay, we are going to do a full rehearsal."* Just as he said that, he notices me walking past. The funny thing is, he stops. Then, he and all of the people sitting at the tables follow my movements, stare at me as I walk past. I smile. Obviously, his mind was not locked into directing his actors and the actor's minds were not locked into their characters.

I continue on my path and went back to the bead shop. I tell my lady the story. She laughs and asks, *"Was that the rehearsal, watching you walk past?"*

The guy, obviously the director, was a chubby, dark-haired guy, in his forties. The people at the tables were all young, blonde, in their early twenties. They obviously had a little bit of money for this production because I'm sure the rental of that restaurant wasn't cheap. His mistake... He fell into the trap of tradition. He wanted to rehearse his actors. But, rehearsals do not work.

I have long understood that you should never rehearse a scene with actors. Why? Because it makes their performance(s) stale. Whenever I'm doing a film, even if we are just testing the lights and sound for camera, and it is the first pass for the actors, I film the scene. The reason for this, oftentimes this first performance is the best—the most natural.

It is like life. Do you get to rehearse life? No, all you can do is live it.

I believe all of us have played scenarios out in our mind, before they ever happen. We play them out the way we want them to occur. But, they are never lived like that. Life takes hold. Each person brings their own, unique personality into the equation, and the situation plays out different than we ever imagined.

So, like true actors acting in a film, all we can do is live life and be in the moment. Though we may pretend to control it, though we may want to rehearse it, we cannot.

Let life be what it is and react to it the way each scene uniquely presents itself. That equals a natural performance, natural freedom.

No rehearsals. They don't work.

You Can Only Play In Your Own Playground

Every now and then I am asked, *"What do I think about Wikipedia?"* Though I don't really think about it at all, I guess, I do have an opinion.

When I first heard about Wikipedia, when it was launched, I thought what a great idea; taking all of the knowledge of everybody and putting it into one place. But, the reality of what has emerged is a bit different. Wikipedia is not based on the knowledge but the opinions of everybody, or more particularly the opinion of a person or persons who is willing to fight to get their ideology at the forefront.

It is an opinion-based website. Not a fact-based source of knowledge—like say a traditional encyclopedia.

For example, I was watching TMZ a few weeks ago and a couple of the people on the show were having a disagreement. One of them immediately put their opinion on Wikipedia and told the other person to look at it.

This illustrates the basis of Wikipedia. Anybody can say anything. And, if it is not challenged, it will remain there as fact.

Way back when it was in its early stages, I was popping around the site one day. I found that Steven Seagal's page was just basically a rip on him. Now, I have no feelings about Seagal one way or the other. I just found that the amount of incorrect and misleading statements that were made on the page was not right. So, I cleaned it up, added some true facts, and so on. I also cleaned up a few other pages, as well.

What I quickly came to find, however, is that there are people on Wikipedia who monitor specific pages and they only want them to reflect the way that they think—whether it is right or wrong.

It is not fact, it is simply the way they see it. And, they will fight to the bitter end to get their point across, even though it may be incorrect.

In fact, if you watch the site, some people are just going around causing all kinds of controversy. I guess that makes them feel alive. I do not know. But, though it may make them feel alive, it does not mean that their actions are justified or necessary.

I think the people who do this are the one's who are not really living life. And, Wikipedia gives them a place to have their voices heard. I mean, if these people were teaching classes, writing books, loving their jobs, raising a family, doing whatever—not only would they not have the time to fight their battles on Wikipedia but they would not care to do so.

Ultimately, I decided, what was the point? I have better things to do with my life than to waste my time and fight meaningless battles on the Internet.

A funny occurrence happened in regard to me, (I guess you can say, in regard to me), on Wikipedia a few years ago.

One of my Black Belt students, from the late 1970s and early 1980s, was contributing to Wikipedia periodically. He contacted me and told me he had been banned from Wikipedia by someone who claimed that he was the same person as somebody else, using different screen names. The funny part of this was, the person who made this accusation, claimed the group of people all contributed to film pages associated with me and particularly to a Zen Filmmaking page.

But, the truth be told, this guy hates my films! And, he only contributed to martial art pages on Wikipedia. In fact, even the accuser said the edits were all made via different editing styles. Whatever that means... But, a Wikipedia administrator, (I guess they are called that), looked through all the contributions and said it was a hard decision to make, but bannered the entire group of five or six contributors. Some who had not been on Wikipedia in years.

What it boiled down to was, the group of banned contributors were all people who had made edits to the page about me on the site. So, the person who started this ruckus was out to jab at me, for whatever reason, not the contributors. How foolish. And, what a waste of time.

Anyway, I am told, two of the banned people made statements that they worked together at some film studio and actually liked my films and my Zen Filmmaking style. Amazing, somebody out there actually likes my movies. ☺

In any case, my friend/student tried to contest the block and got some harsh reprimand from an administrator. He later told me that he looked up the guy's page and the guy had since retired as an administrator as he was going off to college. And, the one who made the judgment was still in high school when it was made. So, these people were in high school when they had been given the task to pass judgment on other people.

Now, I am not saying that teenagers are not competent decision makers. When I was sixteen, I thought I was living like an adult. But, the reality is, until you get out there on your own, are living your own life, and have decided what your life actually is—how can you pass judgment on others?

I have heard in reports on the news, that it has been proven that some of the administrators on Wikipedia have turned out to be as young as thirteen years old.

I mean, what kind of encyclopedia has a thirteen-year-old administrator?

Perhaps the funniest, or most revealing, part of all this is, apparently the administrator who took down the Zen Filmmaking page on Wikipedia was shortly thereafter banned from Wikipedia for using multiple accounts to get their own agenda met. And, another administrator apparently hid the page where the person who worked at the film studio, and dug what I was doing, contested their block.

I am told, you really have to know how to search Wikipedia and get behind these blocks to find this information. So, somebody behind the scenes knew this was all wrong.

As for my student/friend, all he had to do was to set up another account name if he wanted to contribute to Wikipedia again. And, anybody can put another Zen Filmmaking page up on Wikipedia if they want to and are willing to fight for it if they run into this type of situation again.

The point of this discussion... You can only play in your own playground. The world out there is full of children and people with child-like egos who are willing to fight to get their point across. If you go into battle with them, you can fight and you can win. But, what will that mean to your life? Will you be able to accomplish what you really want to accomplish? Or, will you waste all of your Life-Time fighting with people that are not even worth the trouble?

Play in your own playground. Then you have some control.

_____GET OUT OF THE FAST LANE!

Here in California, and I image in other states, as well, when you get a traffic ticket you have the option of going to Traffic School in order to keep it from going on your driving record. As I've had my share of tickets, I've gone to Traffic School a number of times over the years.

Commonly, when the class begins, they go around the room and ask the people what is their pet-peeve in association with driving. Though I have a few, my main one is, GET OUT OF THE FAST LANE!

I mean, don't you hate it when you are driving down a two-lane highway or even on city streets and there is a person in the fast lane either going really slow or going at the exact same speed as the car next to them. From this, there is no way you can get around them.

They do this, and are completely oblivious to the fact that there are other cars on the road. Or, that one is right behind them.

Maybe they don't even care. I don't know. But, I watch and they never look in their rear view mirror.

In every state in this country, there is the slow lane to the right and the passing lane to the left. You are supposed to drive in the slow lane unless you are passing, even if you are going the speed limit. This question is on every driving test. And, everyone has to pass this test to get a driver's license. So, how have people studied and passed the test without knowing this fact? Yet, day-after-day I see people just slow cruising in the fast lane.

What annoys me even more is when these people finally wake up to the fact that they are blocking the flow of traffic and either get out of the fast lane or I pass them in the slow lane; then, they give me a dirty look, like I am doing something wrong.

Last year, I was driving up highway 101 and there was this big burly white pickup truck with large tires on it driving side-by-side with this other car for miles. You would think, with a truck like that, it would driven by some big macho guy driving a hundred miles an hour. But no, he just sat there next to the other car for miles and miles and miles, oblivious to the fact that a line of cars had built up behind him. I was in the lead.

Finally, he sped up and moved over. Then, as if to teach me some sort of lesson, he got right behind me and seriously tailgated me for a few miles. Finally, I pulled out my phone, click on the video camera, and started tapping him. I guess he didn't like that, he backed off.

You know, life is just ridiculous. Unconscious people want to take over all of this Life-Space. And, due to their selfish oblivion, they negatively affect the lives of other people. They do this, and then become angry when someone alerts them to the fact that their inappropriate actions are having a negative effect upon others.

People really need to get away from their selfish, self-serving ways.

If you're not living it, GET OUT OF THE FAST LANE!

Locked Into Your Own Mind

Let's face facts. People live in their own heads—their own minds. You think the way you think. I think the way I think. And, we each think things that only we can understand.

Moreover, each person thinks and experiences you differently than any other person. I mean, how many times have people described you to other people and they were completely wrong? They didn't get YOU at all. Yet, that is how they perceive you. But, another person will hold a completely different impression about you.

Why is this? It is because people base their opinions upon their own perception of reality.

Furthermore, think about how many times you have projected a reality onto something that you expected to happen. You planned to say this, do that, you thought a particular situation would unfold, but the situation never materialized. It was all in your head.

These mind-things are not right or wrong. They are simply the way it is.

But, what this style of mind-stuff behavior does cause in life, is problems. Why? Because each person thinks and they experience life differently—even if they are living in the same place, at the same point in time. From these individualized perceptions, conflict is born.

This may be the reality of life. But, it is a reality that you do not have to take part in or be defined by if you do not choose to be. Why? Because that's the point, your life and your mind is defined by you.

For example, how many times have people asked you, *"What did you mean by that?"* When you thought you were very clear in your statement. Or, how many times have they wondered if you have had an ulterior motive for what you said, and they have thought-and-thought about your words in order to try and figure out their meaning? They did this when you meant exactly what you said, or you meant nothing at all. You just said something.

This goes to the perception of reality, as well. Due to our undying mind-stuff, we each perceive the events that shape our reality in unique manner. Though we may be living at the same point in history, we each are who we are; we each have our own mind. Thus, what happens in our time and space reality is perceived, contemplated, and understood in a manner that is only wholly defined by ourselves.

The fact is, some people are highly delineated by the perceptions that they hold in their mind and they are very locked into their own thought process. They define life by how they see things, what they feel about them, and the definitions that they place upon these perceptions. These people are very locked into their own mind and their own thought process. These are usually individuals who either live a very solitaire life or those who have developed the mindset that they are somehow superior to other people.

There are others, however, who are more open and decide not to be dominated by how they see or perceive life-things, because they understand the transient-ness of life, emotions, desires, and ideologies. In either of these cases, an individual's personality and how they consciously choose to live their life defines their reality.

So, what is the point of this? How locked into your own mind are you? And, how does this effect and affect your reality? It's your mind. Only you can answer this question. How do you want to experience your life?

Stealing and Selling Other People's Work

Ever since the dawning of the Internet, bootlegging, (for lack of a better word), has become quite rampant. Meaning, that people copy and sell products that they did not create to other people for a profit. But, none of that money goes back to the people who actually created the product; be it a book, music, or a film.

Maybe stealing is a better term...

Certainly, the whole Napster syndrome shook the music industry a few years ago. At that point, people were copying music, uploading it, and *"Sharing it"* with other people. Though it changed the music industry forever, it also affected the financial livelihoods of many artists.

In the more recent past, movies have come to be bootlegged, uploaded, and then people are allowed to watch them by paying a price to join the website service that is showing them.

Now, in terms of high budget films, one could argue that the movie studios have already made a lot of money on these films, so why do they need to make more? Be that as it may, there is a whole other side to the issue. For example, people like myself, who pay for their films to be made out of their own pocket. When these sites get a copy of my films and put them up on the Internet, it can really kill sales. And, believe me, it costs a lot of money and time to make a movie. And, it is very sad when someone else is making a profit from my creation, when I am not.

Some people believe that the *"File sharing sites"* are better than the ones just described, as they appear to be free. They are not. Someone in that chain is making money or these sites would not be active. Someone, but not the creator of the project.

Another path where people are commonly bootlegging other people's creations is in relation to books. I have found several of my books, copied and put up on sites on the Internet. Now, let's think about this for a moment. The people who do this may like the book, but they did not write the book, they did not spend the money to have the book printed that was laid out by the publishing company. Yet, they scan the books and are selling people the ability to read them on the Internet. They are the one's making the money. Not the author or the publishing company.

Recently, I was popping around the internet and I found a website that is selling scanned copies of martial art magazines. In fact, this site is selling photocopies of several magazines I wrote articles for. They scan them and then sell them.

Of course, on this website, the people are not honorable enough to provide a name, address, or telephone number where you can contact them. Which illustrates that they know what they are doing is wrong, illegal, and uncool. So, I emailed them. They did not reply.

But, think about this for a moment. How long do you think it takes to write an article? Then, you have to supply photographs for the techniques presented in the article. This all costs time and money.

Back in the day, when these magazines were published, they use to pay me $125.00 per article. The photographs alone used to cost me more than that to produce. So, I personally made no money. And, this is not to mention all the time and money it actually took, on the part of the publishing company, to create and release these magazines. But now, here is somebody on the Internet, who had nothing to do with the creation of these magazines, making money by selling someone else's hard earned work.

Ultimately, if you've ever created something, that you cared about, and took the time and made the effort to get it published or released, you will understand the problem with what is happening when these websites release this information.

We all want things for free or for cheap-er. This being stated, whether you are paying to access a site or viewing and downloading content for free, you really should think about the reality of what is going on and how your actions are affecting the lives of creative people before you access these sites that sell and make money off of the creative work of other people.

_____I'll Have a Scott Shaw

I was having lunch with some friends a few months ago and one of the people ordered an Arnold Palmer. I asked, *"What's that?"* They thought it was very funny that I didn't know what this drink was as it has, apparently, become very well known. They suggested I have one. But, I'm not really a fan of iced tea, even with lemonade, so I declined.

I was having lunch with a friend a couple of days ago and she also ordered an Arnold Palmer. I told her the story; she laughed, and asked, *"What would be the drink if they named one after you?"*

It's kind of funny actually. Since I was a young child I have been concocting drinks. When I was six, I combined ginger ale and grape soda. It tasted so good I was all set to go and trademark it. Of course, I didn't. I was only six.

Then there is vodka with orange and cranberry juice. I came up with that idea in Bangkok back in maybe '84. When I came back to the States, however, I realized this was long before most bartenders had cranberry juice behind the bar. Though it is fairly findable now. So, every now and then I order one.

The only downside of this drink is, you don't taste the vodka so you can tend throw back a few more than you should.

Then there is the always handy extra-large coffee at 711. Add in three mochas and three half-n-half's. Drink it with a straw. That is a drink I accessed many times before hitting out and into the night.

At *Starbucks* I used to drink a Grande, triple shot, heavy crème, latte. That would get my heart rate and my cholesterol going. But, I've since moved onto other drinks at *Starbucks*.

I guess the main drink that I would assign the title of, *"Scott Shaw,"* would be red wine, on the rocks, with two lemon twists.

Normally, if I am having dinner in a restaurant, I will set up with a nice bottle of Italian red wine. But, there is those times when you don't want to drink that much—for whatever reason... In those cases, I order one of the above.

Most waiters have never heard of red wine on the rocks, let alone with two lemon twists, so they tend to give me a bit of a weird look. But, those who come to know me, don't think twice. And, those who have tasted it, tend to like it.

So, next time you need a drink in a bar or restaurant, order a Scott Shaw. ☺

Don't be a Wait-er

First of all, I must preface this with the fact that there is nothing wrong with being a food server if that is what you want to do. I have and have had friends who do this and though they complain about their job like many people, it is an honorable and very necessary profession.

In any case, yesterday morning I was having breakfast at an old-school style restaurant overlooking the ocean. A very nice young man, in his early twenties, was taking care of us. After we had been there awhile another couple came in and they immediate recognized him, remembering him from when he was on a little league team with one of their sons.

Some time passed, as the couple was waiting for more of their group to arrive. Which they did. In walks the aforementioned son, his brother, and their two girlfriends. All were dressed in the pseudo thug, modern street gangster look that is very popular among young Caucasian kids these days. Though this family was obviously very affluent.

With their arrival, the sons immediately begin ripping on and making fun of the guy who had the job as a food server. This began the moment he asked them if he could get them anything to drink. When he came back to our table, he said, *"This is so embarrassing."*

You know, here in L.A., many young people choose the path of being a food server when they are pursuing a career as an actor or actress, as they believe that this job allows them more flexibility to go to auditions. Maybe it does. Also, I have known people who, while going to college, work as food servers in order to make some extra money.

The main point here is that if you want to be a food server, do that. The reality of life is, however, we each set our own course and path for the evolution of our life. Each thing that we do, leads to the next, and the next.

What I have seen is that when people's acting careers didn't take off or once they graduated college, they didn't follow the path of their degree. Then, all that was left for them was the only job they knew, had experience in, and were qualified; that of a food server.

The fact is, it is very hard to change your life course once it has been set.

What I'm saying is, don't be a, *"Wait - er."* Don't wait. Do what you want to do.

No, you are probably not going to go in a be the president of a multinational company on your first day out of high school. But, if that is what you want to do, set a course for that end-goal and pursue a career, and introductory jobs, that will guide you to that end.

Follow your path. Follow your dreams and do not get distracted doing something that you may be, *"Embarrassed"* about just because it pays the bills. There are other jobs out there other than being a waiter to pay the rent.

___What's Wrong with Humanity?

I have just been floored, unable to do much of anything, since I heard the reports of the brutal sexual assault and severe beating that took place against a female international correspondent in Cairo last week. This took place while most of the people were celebrating the stepping down of Mubarak. Out of respect, I am not going to mention her name.

It has made me want to follow the path of Lao Tzu. As legend states, he was so disheartened with society that he simply walked away and went to the wilderness. The problem is, there is no place left to run.

I mean, what is wrong with humanity, for people to do something so devastatingly horrendous to that lady?

Now, this reporter is certainly not the only female that this style of brutality has happened to. But, what her plight has done, is that it has brought this type of treatment to the forefront of the news and the minds of people across the globe.

And, anyone who does this to a woman (or anybody) is just wrong and should be condemned and damned for life. Which I am sure the people who committed that action that will be. But, that does not undo what happened to the reporter or other women who have faced this type of brutality.

I know, from personal experience, that Egypt is not a safe place, especially for women. In 1983, I saved two young naive college exchange students from falling prey to a similar fate. But, perhaps even more disturbing was a year or so later, I had a few hours to kill before my plane took off, so I went to the Cairo Zoo. There were very few people at the zoo that day. I noticed a group of young teenagers walking around. A one point, a fight broke out between two of them. One, a smaller boy and the other one who looked to be one of those kids that had flunked a few grades and was held back, as he was much larger and older. In any case, the moment the fight began, instead of pushing or punching, the larger boy straight-out kicked the smaller boy in the knee. Obviously, the boy fell in pain. Then, instead of embracing his victory, the larger boy started to pull down the pants of the smaller boy. He was obviously going to rape him. I whistled loudly. Seeing me, the group of boys ran away. The injured boy got up, pulled up his pants, and limped away. I'm sure his knee was never the same.

This is something that most westerners do not understand, as here in the west, the definitions of sexuality are fairly clear. There are heterosexuals and there are homosexuals. But, in the Middle East these lines are very blurred. In fact, it is quite common that an older man will have sex with an adolescent or a young male, even though they both may be considered a heterosexual.

But, more to the point, here in the west, adolescence boys get into fights. It happens all the time. There is a winner and there is a loser. But, the loser never anticipates getting sodomized.

The cold hard fact is, the rules are not the same in the middle-east, and many other countries for that matter... But, even here in the U.S., violence against women commonly occurs, as well. And, it is just wrong!

If you've done it. You are wrong. And, you should punish yourself by any means possible.

I mean in life, we have all done things that we know have been wrong. Few of us have, however, done anything of the magnitude that occurred to that reporter in Cairo.

The fact is, in life, we all know what is right and wrong. There is an inner voice that speaks to us. We know what we should or should not do. Some people do not listen to this inner voice, however. Start listening!

Plus, people always attempt to blame their upbringing, their family, their culture, their religion for the wrong things that they do. But, wrong is always wrong. I mean, how much wrong has been done in the name of religion— orchestrated by pundits who program the minds of young people with false ideologies and cause them to hurt other people?

Hurting other people is the ultimate wrong!

Now, I understand that mob mentality played a part in what happened to that reporter. And yes, perhaps she should have taken her own safety more into consideration before venturing out into the crowd. And yes, CBS should have sent a security team with her. But, she did nothing wrong! She was just doing her job. The people that hurt her had no right to overpower a helpless woman. They are the people who did something wrong! And, there should be no forgiveness for their actions.

Growing up where I did, on the sketchy side of L.A., I saw this type of mob mentality all the time. People would never fight you one on one. They would always attack you with their crew, so they had no chance of losing.

And, the reality is, no matter how tough you are, life in not like a Hong Kong Kung Fu movie where the protagonist always emergences victorious. When there is more of them, than there is of you—though you may take few of them with you, you will lose the skirmish. And, this is what happened to that poor reporter. Thankfully a group of women and the military came to her aid before she was killed.

Stop doing wrong things! Make humanity better. Because the world as it is, is fucked up. A better humanity starts with you.

Who's Right?

I went and worked out at a gym I have been going to for over twenty-five years in Huntington Beach this afternoon. When I was done I decided to go and hit the jacuzzi.

I had been relaxing for a few minutes when this African-American woman came into the water and sat down very close to a Vietnamese lady who was sitting next to me.

In this jacuzzi there are numerous jets which shoot out pressured water and people commonly take their place in front of one of these jets. By doing so, each person is allowed to absorb the pressure while having a clearly defined space of their own. The African-American lady didn't do this, however, and had apparently encroached too closely on the Vietnamese ladies space. So, the Vietnamese lady moved, with a look of disgust on her face. The African-American lady then took over her jet.

I observed the situation but just let it go. I then noticed that a place had opened up, where I prefer to sit, so I moved to another jet.

A bit of time passed and then I hear a ruckus. Another Vietnamese lady had become very annoyed at this same African-American woman because there is this one jet, which is very sought after. Why? I really don't really know. But, in any case, people when they are done using it, commonly hand it off to a friend or an older person. In this case, the Vietnamese lady was giving it to an older Vietnamese lady but the African-American lady had apparently slide into the spot as it was being handed off.

The Vietnamese lady said, *"I was giving this to her."* The African-American lady, in all her *bravada*, shaking her head from side to side, said, *"I don't care bitch. I want it."*

Now, neither of these women were young. For you may expect this type of behavior from a youth. In fact, they were both, at least, in their mid-forties; probably older.

In any case, the Vietnamese lady looks at me, as if seeking some sort of assistance. She said, *"I am just trying to be kind to this old lady. You understand?"* I shook my head yes.

Then, she started to speak to me in Vietnamese. Though I have a very rudimentary understanding of the language, the nuisances go past me. But, I did understand that she then apologized to the older Vietnamese woman for not being able to give her the sought after jet. This, as the black woman sat there in all her power, conquest, and arrogance.

I mean, how could anyone feel comfortable sitting there, at that jet, after this situation had occurred? Yet, she sat there.

So, who was right? I mean this situation is so definitive of life and how people attempt to overpower others in order to get their own way and meet their own desires.

You have got to understand, if you live your life like this, taking from others and being rude, you will forever meet resistance, people will not like you, and you will continually encounter negative events, because that is what you are unleashing. From this, you will have a life defined by battles in which there is always a winner and a loser. And, sooner or later you will lose. Just as in the gun-fighting days of the old west, there will always be somebody faster.

But, more than that, being nice, kind, and generous, is just better. I mean, what does taking something from somebody else really mean? For example, how did snaking that jet from the old lady really make that woman's life any better? And, how can she even feel comfortable with herself at her victory?

We have all met people like this. Do we like them? No, we do not. Nobody does.

Just be nice and the world instantly becomes a better place.

_____Anybody Can Do That!

I believe that we all have seen, in television shows and in movies, when an actor walks into an art gallery, sees a piece of abstract art, and makes the statement, *"Anybody can do that."* But, can they? Maybe you have heard a similar statement in an art gallery or museum. I know I have.

Here is the difference. The people that are creating the works of art, actually doing it, are the artists. They are the one who are envisioning the idea and bringing that idea to life: be this in painting, drawing, music, film, photography, or any other form of art. The people who are making the aforementioned statement are not doing it. They are not an artist. They do not have the inclination or the passion for creating art. So no, they cannot do it.

Even if a person, who made this statement, would actually go, buy paint, a canvas, and then paint what they consider abstract art, that would not be art. That would simply be mimicking the art of another person.

Art is created by someone who has a vision to bring a particular subject matter to life. This is why the work of an artist, though forever evolving, follows a continually similar path in its presentation. Each piece has a refined and specific look and feel. And, though they may appear, *"Doable,"* by, *"Anybody,"* they are not done by anybody. They are created by the person who has a particular vision that they want to bring to life. That is an artist.

Trying

The reality of life is that we all want to accomplish something. As someone who has been involved with the various aspects of spirituality for virtually my entire existence, there has been the constant mantra—we should desire nothing.

It is claimed that desiring nothing is the most straightforward path to universal awareness. Be that as it may, the reality is, even desiring nothing, is desiring something. And we, as human beings, each desire to achieve something.

Certainly, throughout our lives, these desires change. But, nonetheless, desiring a desired outcome, an accomplishment, is a constant.

Some of our desires are more selfish and self-serving, while others are more benevolent; in that some of us want to help others. But, desire for accomplishment and achievement is the constant.

This is not bad or good. It is simply life.

From a personal perspective, there are two types of people who commonly contact me, in regard to desire and accomplishment. The first are those who want me to help them achieve something. The second are those who have achieved something and want to show me their accomplishment.

Both are fine. They are simply different sides of the same coin.

But, the point is, in life, those who have achieved something, done something, created something, have actualized their dream. They have followed the course and have accomplished and completed their end-goal. The rest of the people are left in a constant state of desire, having achieved nothing.

Not achieving is the place where individual lies about accomplishments are born. This is where you find the people who tell untruths about what they have not achieved. These lies are based on what they have not done and what they still hold the desire to have accomplished and achieved.

On the other side are those who have followed their desire and have achieved. These people can say, *"I did it! This creation is mine."*

So, here's the key to life and to desire fulfillment, TRY. Because if you try, you have done something. If it doesn't work out, change your approach, and try again; because trying equals accomplishment.

Everybody, (for example), wants to be the biggest movie star, the biggest rock star, the biggest rap star, the biggest real estate mogul, greatest professor, philanthropist, whatever... They want someone to discover them and hand them the keys to the kingdom, simply because they are who they are. But, this is not realistic.

Though the biggest and best may be not be a realistic desire, you can still work towards this end and be happy with the progress and the accomplishment you make in this quest. For in this modern digital age, anybody can be anything. That is the reality.

Though you may not be the biggest, you can create your goal product: be it a movie, music, a book, whatever, and get it out there. This will equal that you will have accomplished your desires, and you will have made something of yourself.

My advice is that you stop waiting for someone to do it for you. Do it yourself.

Sure, it may not be easy. But, you can accomplish. All you have to do is try.

Trying is the key to fulfillment.

The Martial Arts

As someone who has been involved with the martial arts for virtually my entire life, I can say with authority that if someone desires to learn the techniques, anyone can make the martial arts a part of their life. But, as in all other elements of life, you must do what you do consciously. You must think about what you are doing and why you are doing it. Or, you may muddy-up the waters for others.

My father was a black belt who earned his rank during his service in the military during World War II. My uncle was a professional boxer prior to World War II. Me, I began formally studying when I was six years old. That was over forty-five years ago. So, the refined fighting arts have been a part my entire life.

Now, I am not saying that myself or anyone else who studies the martial arts, for however long, will be the perfect technician of all techniques. But, that is what I consider mastery; that is the ultimate statement—knowing what you can do and then focusing on that, and doing it well.

Something that I find amusing is that since the dawning of the age of the internet, there has been a certain group of nameless/faceless people who feel that they have the ability and the right to cast judgment on martial art styles and other martial artists; attempting to either give them props and/or discredit them, and then spread their thoughts to the masses. The problem is, who are these people who are casting judgment? And, what gives them the right and the privilege to judge anyone?

In life, we are all drawn to who and what we are drawn to. We like what we like, and we dislike what we dislike. But, most of these ideologies are based upon social programming, not upon fact. This is a subject that I have addressed in so many of my articles and books.

The problem with the martial arts, and the fighting arts in general, is that they are based upon the concept of conquest—of who can beat whom. But, this beating, (or winning), is no longer solely based upon physical prowess, as it may have been in centuries gone past. Instead, in this modern age, it is based upon who said what; based upon what lies, preconceived impressions, and misrepresentation they use to present their case.

For this reason, martial art websites and discussion groups have popped up, spewing all kind of falsities and non-facts about martial artist and martial art styles in general. Instead of relying upon facts and the truth, all they disseminate are preconceived opinions.

I guess I should write, OPINIONS in capital letter. Why? Because if you are judging the techniques and the ideologies of others, that means that you no longer have anything to learn. If you have nothing more to learn, that means that you are an absolute master. Are you?

Think about this for a moment before you finalize any judgment on a martial art style or a martial artist. Think about who you are, what you have learned, how long you have been doing it, and if you possess the right, through time and through trail, to judge anyone.

Remember, the martial arts are an art. You need to think about them like an art form. You may like a certain style of art; you may dislike another style of art. But, in either case, that does not mean that it is not art. You may like a certain style of music, you may dislike another, but that does not mean that it is not music.

Born in the U.S.A.

United States politics has always been full of rhetoric. In the American political system, people win and people lose. This causes individuals to form conspiracy theories and to tell untruth in order to get people to listen to their point of view in an attempt to put their ideas and ideals at the forefront.

Since the election of President Barak Obama, there has been a certain segment of the U.S. population that has not liked his victory and have attempted to unseat him. One of the methods they have used is to claim that he was not born in the U.S.A. The people that embrace this path are commonly referred to as, *"The Birthers."*

But, let's think about this for a moment. President George W. Bush was the President of the United States before Barak Obama. Bush is a republican and Obama is a democrat. George W. Bush is the son of former President, George H. W. Bush—who, among other things, was also, prior to his presidency, the head of the C.I.A. Now, many people, including former President Bill Clinton, who made the statement, *"He had to cheat to win,"* believe that George W. Bush manipulated his way into the presidency. Nonetheless, he was a two-term President of the United States of America.

Here's the question: Between the power of investigation that George W. Bush possessed, and the power that his father, in association with the C.I.A. held, can anyone believe that if it were true that Barak Obama was not actually born in Hawaii, that this information would not have somehow amazingly, anonymously, and secretly been revealed before a democrat would have been allowed to win the election?

_____Don't Cry Over Spilled...

I was having dinner in an Italian restaurant in San Francisco's North Beach last Saturday night when my lady, while reaching across the table, spilled her drink. We have all done this at some point in our lives and it is really no big issue. A restaurant employee quickly came to our rescue and wiped up the spilled Mojito.

The restaurant we were in was similar to all the restaurants in North Beach on a Saturday night, in that it was very crowded, and the tables are very close together.

With the spilled drink, my lady and I began laugh. In our joy, I looked over to a woman sitting at the table next us and smiled. Instead of returning the smile, she glared at me. If looks could kill...

Now, here is the issue with existence and something to look at in order to define how you interact with life. People are either happy or they are not. People either choose to make all life events a unique experience or they choose to make them a crisis.

In this case, the spilled drink did nothing to alter this woman's life, but she chose to make it a crisis—a means to define and alter the rest of her evening and perhaps the rest of her life. This is something to think about when you decide how to react to all life situations.

As for my lady and I... I ordered her another Tequila Mojito and, for myself, I ordered another Chianti on the rocks with two lemon twists. We continued to smile.

How Quickly We Forget

President Obama gave a speech today concerning the turmoil that is taking place in Egypt. First of all, as someone who has spent a lot of time in Egypt, I know, first-hand, that the need for an improved democracy is imperative in order for that country to move forward into the rest of the twenty-first century. For this reason, I am one hundred percent behind the revolution that is taking place.

To Obama's speech... In it, he stated that the need to protest without governmental interference is imperative and this right should be allowed to the Egyptian people. Certainly, I agree with this point. But, as he said that, I could not help but to think back to just a few decades ago, when here, in the United States, protestors were commonly beaten by police and killed by the National Guard simply for protesting against various aspects of the government and, most particularly, against the Vietnam War.

Think about this, because I believe many people do not remember. Young people were drafted when they were eighteen years old and sent into military service. At that point in U.S. history, a person couldn't even vote until they were twenty-one. This meant that our youth could and would die for this country but could not vote for who was president. Does that seem right?

How many young Americans died and/or were disabled for life in service to a war that proved nothing? I knew a few.

But, back to the main point. Commonly, when people would protest, the police would come in with their billy-clubs swinging. They would proudly bloody heads, break bones, and knock people out. Then, they would often times cut the hair of the protestors, just to make some kind of moralistic statement. This was America in the 1960s and 1970s.

President Obama is just a few years younger than I. So, I am certain he remembers this era, vividly. And, no doubt, he too must have encountered prejudice and repression during this period of time.

Myself, I remember going into restaurants when I was in high school, during the 1970s, and my friends and I would not even be served simply because we had long hair. And, this was in Los Angeles. It must have been much worse in other parts of the country. And, that is just one example of the meaningless prejudice I experienced in that era.

Certainly, America has changed. But, many of the people who lived through that era are still alive. People are alive who lived on both sides of the issues. Those, like myself, who fought to change the path of this country and those who attempted to keep it locked in the dark ages.

Though United States attempts to be the moral compass for the world, it must be remembered where we came from. It must be known who we were only a few decades ago. Because though it is very easy to pass judgment on what we feel is right and wrong in the world, we must not forget the lives that were lost and damaged due to who America was and, in some cases, still is.

Racial Slurs

I was watching T.V. last night when a commercial came on. The first words spoken were from an Asian lady who said, *"Don't call me a Chink."* Next came the various other minority races, *"Don't call me a Spick." "Don't call me a Diaper Head." "Don't call me a Kike." "Don't call me a Nigger."* And, so on. What I found surprising was that there was no Caucasian saying, *"Don't call me a Honkey."*

As someone who grew up initially in a predominately African-American community and then a primarily Latin community, I am one of the few Caucasians who have actually experienced this scenario from the other side of the issue.

When I was in grammar school, there wasn't a day that went by that someone didn't call me a Honkey or a White Paddy. And, as I have told the story before, the day Martin Luther King Jr. was assassinated, as the only Caucasian kid in my grammar school, the local Junior High School gang planned to come and kill me at the end of the school day. The word was out; my classmates kept coming up to me, with smiles on their face, telling me, *"They're going to get you Honkey."* I was obviously scared. At the end of the day, I left the school and was planning to hurry home, but as I turned the corner to walk home, there they came, a large number of African-American teenagers. They were coming for me. I ran back to the school. Luckily, the police had heard about the situation, as well. They drove me home, as they gang yelled racial slur and threats at me. I never returned to that school.

My Junior High School years were also plagued with racial violence, against Caucasian people, but I won't go into that here. So yes, I have experienced racial prejudice, even though I am white.

Some may say the white people deserve it as they repressed the other races in the United States. But, I never did any of that. Why should I be the one to be blamed, simply for the color of my skin? On the other side of the coin, I am sure this is the way many people of color have felt throughout the years, as well.

In recent years it also has become very politically incorrect to ever mention that there is racism against white people. But, all you have to do is travel into any ethnic community in the U.S. or anywhere in the western world for that matter and you will hear it.

When I was young, for me, racial slurs were simply a by-product of life. They were said to me. Everybody said them and most people would think nothing of them. I heard white people speaking to them about other races. And, due to my environment, I continually heard black people saying them, as well. That was just the way it was. Everybody did it.

When you were angry or frustrated with someone you may refer to that person with a detrimental term. It may be something like, *"Asshole."* Or it may have been racial. This was simply a way to define them. This was not right. But, I don't think it necessarily made a person a racist. It simply gave them a context for separating themselves from another individual.

But, no matter what the type of definitive terms used, is this manner of speech hurtful? Yes it is.

The other side of the issue is that some people are very proud of their race. I believe this is the most important element of this equation.

In today's world, it is very common, in films and in music, for African-Americans to refer to each other as, *"Niggas."* It is; it has become a term of endearment. But, that only works on a black-to-black level. Another example is that if you call someone a, *"Honkey,"* some people will reply, *"That's right! I am white."* And, they are very proud of it. And, this goes across all of the racial spectrum. Many people define themselves by their race and are very proud of being just whom and what they are.

Ultimately, every word is defined solely by the ears of the person or persons who hears it. As times change and this world become more and more multiracial, all of the races will merge and there will be only one race. Then, these racial slurs will be gone, but I am sure new derogatory terms will rise into usage. People simply want to be more than others. They want to set themselves apart as something bigger and better. Right or wrong, does not exist. It is simply the way of humanity. For I am sure, even the people who spoke the words in that commercial have their own unique prejudices—their own unique sense of self and superiority. For better or for worse, this is life. This is humanity. As individuals we can continually attempt to be more and raise ourselves above the limits of the lower-mind. But, at the end of the day we are trapped by whatever body we find ourselves in. Love it or leave it…

Fractured

As media has taken control, it is continually detailed how so many of the world's people are psychologically messed up, damaged, fractured. I do not believe that this is a new phenomenon. I am sure that it has been going on since the dawn of humanity. It is simply that due to the fact that we live in this age of information and media, all of the things that take place, all of the abstract psychologically conditions of the people, are broadcast to the masses.

Each of us encountered psychological trauma in our life. I do not believe that there is anyone who has not encountered some life-changing event that altered us for the worse. All-be-it that we can now more freely speak about these events, in our currently place in time, than those of times gone past. But, none-the-less, that does not mean that these events do not change the course of our lives.

As I have long written, we can take any of these events and turn the bad to good, simply by the way we view them. Combine this with all of the psychotherapy that is out there and available, we should all be FINE. But, we are not.

The reality of psychological trauma is, some people simply deal with it better than others. This is a completely personality-based reality. Some people are simply born with a better ability to cope than others. Sure, mental, spiritual, psychological training, and even medical drug-based prescriptions can help people overcome the negative elements that have occurred in their life, but in many cases, all these mental, spiritual, or psychological techniques do is to teach people how to better cover up the pain.

For example, religion is all about dismissing. It is all about repression. *"God was testing you." "You survived. Obviously god loves you. So, move on."* And, so on.

Psychoanalysis, on the other hand, is all about getting to the source of a feeling. The problem with psychoanalysis and therapy, in general, is that it only presents a situation from a very limited, very singularly, personal perspective. One person is telling their shrink what they feel, how they feel, and what they think about a subject. As the client is, in essence, the employer of the shrink, how much truth is the psychologist going to tell a paying client?

Speaking of truth... People lie all the time! Who is to say what they tell their shrink is not an alteration of the truth? From this, how can any true therapy-based realization be gained?

Then, there is the medical drug-based cover up of pain, depression, and the like. A drug may make you feel better. But, a drug is a drug is a drug... Drugs only mask the pain. So, again, just like religion, they are based in repression.

The reality is, people are damaged. They may be damaged by their family, their friends, their society, their priest, or someone they do not even know. As most of us are damaged, life is simply about figuring out how to deal with that damage and make it through—try to make the best of the cards you were dealt. Whatever works for you, (as long as you are hurting no one else and exacerbating the world situation), who can truly judge that it is wrong?

I truly wish it were different. I truly wish we weren't all hurt. But, we are...

The Party

Once upon a time, I dedicated one of my novels to my friend Venchinzo, with the caption, *"To Venchinzo, my bro, who like I, refuses to ever grow old and stop the party."*

In any case, he and I, we did party hard. But, by the time we were in our early forties, it had just gotten old; hittin' the bars and clockin' the hoes. The crowds had become a decade or two younger than us and the drunk driving laws became very stick. Our time was at hand.

Very few have the temperament to find enlightenment at bars and in dance clubs through the bottom of the beer mug. It is an art form. It is a path that can only be transversed by a very few. But, that is exactly what we did.

As the story goes; me, I always had a main and central babe strapped up crib-side to return home to after our nights of debauchery. Venchinzo reunited with his first serious girlfriend, twenty years after they had first met, and they had a baby. I was happy for him. It was something he had always wanted.

The last time we really hit out to the night was about a decade ago. His girlfriend's mother was watching the kid, and we moved out to the night. The first stop, via his request, was his old apartment in Venice. His apartment building mates were not inspired by his arrival, however. They had places to be and though he protested, they literally told him he had to leave. These actions really showed me a lot about the truth of friendship, (or acquaintance-ship), and how it plays out in life.

It was so much like the middle stages of the Burt Lancaster film, *The Swimmer*. Though this is a very obscure film, it is so depictive of life. The lead character decided that he was going to swim every pool in his affluent neighborhood. He starts out, everybody is happy to see him, and loves him. As he moves forward, people are less-and-less pleased by his presence. By the end of the film, no one wants him around, until he finally returns home to find his family has left him and he is locked out of his house in the pouring rain.

In any case, next, we hit a couple of the old haunts. The bars had changed, however. No longer were they atmospheric. Now, they had become nothing but trendy.

We finally made our way to the *Good Luck Bar* in Hollywood; right at the junction of Hollywood and Sunset Boulevard.

For the record, if Venchinzo was drinking beer, he could drink with the best of them all day and all night. Add the hard stuff to the mix, and the story changes. As this was something we had begun doing a few stops before our arrival at this place, Venchinzo was toasted.

He went to the restroom. As he returned to the bar, he forgot there was a step onto the main floor of the establishment and literally tripped and stumbled into the bar. Without losing a beat, he ordered another round. The bartender, intelligently, turned him down.

And, that was that. The end of an era. As in all cases of life; change happens...

We had trouble finding our way back to his place as he had moved from Venice Beach to this duplex in the central city portion of L.A. Venchinzo had passed out. I was driving my '64 Porsche 356 SC trying to navigate and remember where he actually lived. It took me quite a while as I was quite drunk, as well.

When I finally figured it out, his girlfriend was very mad that he had gotten drunk. She blamed it on me. Sure, whatever...

They eventually broke up and he took possession of the kid. He became a single father. He quit his long-standing job at a bank, thinking he would be a bartender. That didn't work out. Then, due to the recession of the twenty-first century, (the decline of western civilization that I had seen coming, literally, since I was in grammar school), he hit hard times, and went from job to job when he could even find them.

For a couple of decades, we hung out all the time, charting the realms of drunken enlightenment; experienced on the inner-city streets of Los Angeles—detailed for those few who can actually walk this path to *Samadhi* in some of my poetry and novels. But now, I haven't seen him in a few years. The last couple of times were at his brother, Saturday Jim's, fiftieth birthday party and his mother's seventieth.

This is the reality of life, the party does stop. By hook or by crook; times change, people change, life changes, and we are each forced to find new pathways to *Satori*.

_____Keith and Kenny

When I was in kindergarten two distinct gangs emerged. Yes, we were five years old, and two gangs were formed and existed in my class. One was headed by a boy named Keith and the other by a boy named Kenny. Keith was a stocky lad. Kenny, on the other hand, was very tall—much taller, by a foot or so, than the rest of the boys in our class.

There were core affiliations for each of these crews. As in older gangs, the kids would define themselves by which clique they were associated with. *"I'm in Kenny's gang."* Or, *"I'm in Keith's gang."* Where all this gang-stuff came from, I don't even know. Probably from older brothers and stuff. I mean we were five years old!

In any case, Keith was one of those obnoxious little boys. He always wanted to play the game, *"Look up. Look Down. Look at my finger."* Then, he would flip your nose with his finger. It really bothered me. I told my father. He said, *"Next time he does it, punch him in the nose."*

The next day at school, Keith comes up to me, *"Look up. Look down."* But, this time, the outcome was different. Bam, I punched him in the nose. He stood there crying and crying, holding his nose. That was the outcome of my first fistfight.

The principal came up. As any kid would be, I was very worried about the repercussions. He just smiled at me. *"Everything Okay,"* he asked. I guess he had heard about the antics of Keith. There were no repercussions.

I didn't realize it, nor had I even attempted to do it, but I had defeated the leader of the gang.

The kids in Keith's gang all stood around watching him cry. I was the one to punch him, they all now looked to me for guidance. But, I had none to give. I didn't want the responsibility. I just wanted to be a five-year-old in kindergarten who wrote love notes and put them in this one girl's lunch box that I liked.

This is the point. People want to belong. That is why they congregate and join gangs. That is why they join political parties or religious groups—which are pretty much just the same as a gang. They just have a different focus for their desired domination. People want to be told that they are doing the right thing, that they are a part of the greater good, that they are wanted and needed. But, here are the questions, who are you? Are you who you are? Or, are you defined by those around you? Do you need other to prove that you are what you think you are? Or, are you whole and complete onto yourself?

There is no right or wrong answer. Simply a question that you should be able to answer.

Drama Queen

Have you ever noticed that some people just create chaos wherever they go? They stick their nose in everybody else's business. They talk behind people's backs. The say that, this person said that, when they did not. They just simply create drama wherever they go.

People like this are truly lacking from within. This is a psychological condition, just like so many other things and other elements of life. But, more than that, it is a choice. People choose to behave in this manner. It is just like the child who cries and screams until they get what they want—some/many people never outgrow this learned behavior. They have found that if they stir up the pot enough people will become interactive and get mad, angry, sad, hurt, whatever. What the person who behaves like this has gained, (just like the child who screams long enough) is that take control over the situation. From this, the feel fulfilled/they feel that they are something more than what they actually are, they fell that they are something better. But, in reality this is not the case.

People who behave like this may control the moment of a person; they may take control over their emotions for a second but in the end all they do is hurt themselves. Why? Because at the end of the day they treat everyone like this. So, even the people that they consider friends, sooner or later, end up on the receiving end of this behavior.

Moreover, it is very easy in life to become addicted to adrenalin. We all want fun, excitement, and to be fulfilled. For most of us, we find this via normal channels, whether it is spending time with our family, paying sports, running, doing hatha yoga, going to a concert, or whatever. For those who have a misplaced understanding of life and adrenal flow, the seek stimulation from faulty, negative sources; i.e. wrongful interaction with other people.

People who exist and live their lives at this level always end up destroying themselves. This occurs, first of all, because of the fact that the, *"Real,"* people of the world, those who are actually successful, competent, or creative, do not wish to associate with this type of person. This is due to the simply reason that they do not need all the melodrama in their life. For those who do choose to associate with this style of person, they too eventually become disenchanted and move away. Because those they may initially be drawn to the adrenalize lifestyle; where everything ends in crisis, they too eventually fall victim and realization that association with this type of person can only bring detriment to their life.

Ultimate, when you watch this type of person following through with their life-actions, it is obviously that they are on a conclusion course with the destiny of the karma they have created From this, they will fall and they will fall hard. When you see them enacting their behavior, time-and-time again, it is obvious what will be the outcome; personal disaster.

As in all cases, we are born with a personality; we are schooled and trained by family, society, culture, and personal desires. At then end of the day, it is we who choose to what we will do with all of the influential elements.

Do you want to live a conscious, focused, create life? Or, do you want to be a Drama Queen bringing havoc to all those you encounter and eventually destroying your own life?

The Commune

When I was in my first year of college, I had rented a small apartment near the campus. There were several other young people living in the building. We were all budding musicians; so we would often take out our guitars, sit down, turn up our amps, and play rock n' roll—disturbing the older residence of the building.

I had recently returned from my first trip to India and, as such, was still wearing the orange-colored clothing of the *sanyass* order of which I was an initiate. As most of the people couldn't get their tongue around my full Sanskrit name, they all just called me, "Swami."

A new couple moved into the building. He was a guitarist and worked as a carpet layer. She was piano player who worked as a dental assistant. Both were very nice.

Virtually the first time I met them, the girl inquired and found out that I had a Fender Rhodes electric piano in my apartment. She immediately invited herself up. No problem...

Once in my apartment she tinkled the ivories for a few minutes and then set her sights on me. Never let it be said that I am one to turn down a beautiful woman. Within a few minutes we were making love. I worried that her husband may come knocking. But, he never did.

This periodic relationship went on for a time. Then, after they had lived in the building for a few months, he, (the husband), suggested that we, (the musicians and other young friends who lived in the building) all rent this nearby ranch together. As this was the San Fernando Valley that had only a few decades the previous been the farming area of Los Angeles, there were still a lot of very large properties in the area. He promised it would be this Rock n' Roll utopia. Everybody agreed, except me. I knew there would be problems.

I continued living in my apartment, pursuing my education and teaching the martial arts and yoga. I would often visit what I joking called, *"The Commune."* There: Sex, Drugs, Rock n' Roll, and various other forms of debauchery were quite prevalent. But then, the shit hit the fan. The husband collected all the rent money from everyone and bailed; leaving his wife and everybody else totally screwed. They were all evicted, and nobody had anywhere to go.

One guy, (a person I had been friends with for quite some time), I drove up to the mountains above Bakersfield to live with his father and his father's thirteen-year-old girlfriend; who he claimed to the authorizes, was his daughter. But, that's another story. My friend's wife had left him and moved back in with his patents. So, he brought with him his ex-biker chick girlfriend, (the reason his wife left him), who was also living at the ranch and had nowhere else to go. She was sixteen. He was twenty-two. In doing this, however, he completely alienated another one of our close friends who was also totally in love with the ex-biker chick girl. You see the mess?

One of the guys just faded away. As he was originally from Philadelphia and had no family in L.A., he was destitute. Sometime later, I saw him begging for money at a truck stop near Bartow, California when I was driving to Las Vegas. He was so out of it, he didn't even recognize me. I gave him a fin ($5.00).

The moment the husband bailed, the piano player, dental hygienist girl called me—though she played all the games of romance, she had summoned me solely to have sex. I guess she wanted to get back at her husband. All good, this had been going on for quite some time between us by this point.

Had the next event not taken place, I may well have given her a place to live while she got her life back on track. But, instead of ending her *"Get even with her husband,"* scenario with me, she then had sex with all the other guys in the house before they were kicked out. And, some of them were pretty disgusting and very sleazy.

Her actions sure made me feel really special!

The last time I saw her was just before the police came to kick them out. She was totally broken. I took her for a motorcycle ride on a cool spring night. We stopped to talk. She said I made her feel better. A few weeks later I heard she killed herself.

You see, this is the problem with life. People do what they do, thinking it will make them feel better. But, it does not. People do what they do, but very few every live their life from a place of consciousness. They just exist, driven forward by desire. So, people cheat, they steal, they have sex with whomever, whenever; and in the process, they destroy their own karma and the lives of other people. And, people are fragile. They break.

This is life. You need to think about what you're doing, why you are doing it, and whom else you are affecting by doing what you are doing.

_____Monkey Wrench in the Gears

Life goes along for most of us quite expectedly. We do what we do. And, though we may not always be *Thriving*, we are *Surviving*. Most of life is Okay.

Then, out of the blue we are hit with an unexpected sucker punch to the back of the head. Something goes really wrong. This may occur on all kinds of levels: interpersonal, mechanical, or a natural disaster. From this, a monkey wrench really gets thrown into the gears of our life and everything becomes a mess.

First of all, this is JUST life. Like the only saying goes, *"Shit happens."* No one is immune. The more involved and complicated your life, however, the more chance you have of having a monkey wrench thrown into your gears. On the other hand, the less you do, the less chance you have of unexpected occurrences.

This is why the *Tao Te Ching* states, *"To the man of the world, everyday something is acquired. To the man of Tao, everyday something is lost."*

By consciously stepping away from the world and the ways of the world, not only does your life become more passive and clearer, it also becomes less prone to obstacles. But, the reality is; life is life. We all seek our own form of involvement. We all need human interaction. And, we all need to do THINGS. From these things is where chaos is born.

So, what is the answer? Many on the spiritual path continually attempt to step farther and farther away from the world. But, as a living being, we are all going to die. This too is a monkey wrench in the gears. Because, we each have things we would like to accomplish, complete, actualize, or witness at the time of our death. This is one of the primary curses of life. If we continually step away, attempting to refine ourselves to the degree that we believe we are free from consequences; all that will be had is life left unlived and a death full of regrets.

The trick, the key if you will is to be able to step back from any crisis that befalls you. Don't attribute it to god testing you or destiny attempting to make your stronger. Just see it for what it is. A Life-Thing.

Then when it happens, do what you just to get your life back on track.

Don't make this process a big ordeal! Just do it. Take what comes. Do what your must. Make the decisions you must make, guided by the choices that are laid out in front of you. Forgive if you have to. Forget if you must. And, move on, the best you can. Because believe me, this is life, there will always be monkey wrenches thrown in your gears.

www.ingramcontent.com/pod-product-compliance
Lightning Source LLC
Chambersburg PA
CBHW070728160426
43192CB00009B/1361